In Different Waters

May 2013

To Hope, I hope that you enjoy the book.

Best wishes
Ruth Gonyaw

an autobiography
Ruth Gonyaw

In Different Waters

TATE PUBLISHING
AND **ENTERPRISES**, LLC

Published by Tate Publishing & Enterprises, LLC
127 E. Trade Center Terrace | Mustang, Oklahoma 73064 USA
1.888.361.9473 | www.tatepublishing.com

Tate Publishing is committed to excellence in the publishing industry. The company reflects the philosophy established by the founders, based on Psalm 68:11,
"The Lord gave the word and great was the company of those who published it."

Book design copyright © 2013 by Tate Publishing, LLC. All rights reserved.
Cover design by Jan Sunday Quilaquil
Interior design by Mary Jean Archival

Published in the United States of America

ISBN: 978-1-62510-304-8
1. Biography & Autobiography / Adventurers & Explorers
2. Travel / Mexico
13.04.01

Dedication

To Brittnay and Trenton with much love.

Acknowledgements

My love and a big Thank you to all our friends and family for trying to understand us.

Tom Gonyaw for helping us choose a boat.

Kevin Stolz (www.creativesolutions.com.mx) for your constant and tireless assistance throughout our endeavor.

Hannah Morales for caring , helping, and worrying about us.

Elvia Morales for helping us with our accounting and attorney problems, and being our friend.

Raul for always taking good medical care of us and for getting me out of jail.

My sister Dale Wildman, now deceased, for her love, worries and care.

Karen Gillespie, Leslie Gillespie-Darrow, Judy Ransom, and Kay York for without you I wouldn't have been able to come home and trail ride, go to Quarter Horse Congress or the Arab Nationals, have a place to stay, wonderful care for my horse nor a vehicle to use while I was back in Michigan.

Carol and Bob Kemp and Cheryl and Garnett Todd for pushing our tour and your caring friendship.

Contents

Introduction

I have often thought and have also told many people that what my daughter, Laurel and I tried and accomplished was hopefully *the* most difficult thing that God has planned for us while we are here on earth. However, if it is not, I know that he will give us the strength to complete whatever new task or tasks that we are supposed to complete. What is this thing I am talking about, you ask? Well, let me tell you our story. This story consists of quite a few people, but the main characters are: myself (Ruth), my daughter, Laurel, my granddaughter, Brittnay and my grandson, Trenton. This is written as best that I can remember.

Throughout my telling of our story, I will be referring to certain people as our angels watching over us. There are also many coincidences that happened along the way. I have a quote on my refrigerator that states, "Coincidence is when God chooses to remain anonymous." I truly believe this.

The Vacation

It all started when I decided that I wanted to go on a Caribbean vacation. I was undecided between Jamaica or Cancun, Mexico. I had never been to either, so when I consulted a travel agent, she highly recommended Cancun. I called my daughter, Laurel, and invited her to go with me as my husband of thirty years did not like to travel unless it was in a 4×4 to go hunting or fishing in the north country of Michigan. I would tell people, "It is against his religion to go south of our town." Laurel, of course, was thrilled at the prospect!

In February of 1996, Laurel and I packed our bags and headed south for Cancun, Mexico! We were very excited and could not wait to get there! However, we had a major problem arrive almost as soon as we landed upon Mexican soil. When you arrive, as in any foreign country, you have to stand in line to get through customs. The lines were very long; it seemed to take forever, but we were finally next in line. I handed my papers in first and got through with no problem. However, when Laurel handed the customs officer her papers, her birth certificate was not in the papers! I had kept everything in an orderly manner, having put each person's papers in their own special Ziploc bag. Laurel had asked to see hers on the plane to look through them, so when her birth certificate was not in the packet, we thought that perhaps she had dropped it on the plane. I came back through, and I waited downstairs, hoping that maybe it would turn up while she ran upstairs and back to the gate where we had arrived. By the time she got there, no one was around that spoke any English. She was in a complete panic, and she finally found someone who spoke English. She explained what had happened and what we were thinking that perhaps she had dropped it on the plane. They would not allow her to go back onto the plane to check; however, they said they would look on the floor of the plane and also check the garbage bags for it. Eventually, someone came back off the plane and told Laurel that her birth certificate could not be found anywhere. They told her that she was going to have to stay there and would have to return to the United States on the return flight since she did not have the proper ID to get into Mexico. While that was going on upstairs, I was waiting downstairs for what seemed like hours! As I was standing against the wall, watching everyone going through customs and ready to have a great time, I was also very panic-stricken, wondering what in the world had happened to Laurel. The immigration officer that had tried to check us through came up to me and handed me Laurel's birth certificate. He told me that apparently, she had dropped it while waiting in the line; someone eventually spotted it lying on the floor and turned it in. I thanked him profusely and rushed upstairs to try to find Laurel. When I found her, she was bawling her eyes out, and I had a horrible migraine, but we were both okay. We claimed our baggage, and then we started looking for someone from Apple Tour. Soon we were on our way to our hotel in a van. The trauma was over, and we were ready to start our vacation. We absolutely fell in love with the Caribbean and the Mexican people as well.

If you have never seen the Caribbean, the different shades of blues and greens are breathtaking. The waves come crashing in on the lovely white sand that is always cool to your feet. The Mexican people that we came in contact with all seemed so happy and very pleasant. Music was always playing everywhere we went. *One day, we went out on a catamaran and had a great time.* We both had always loved sailing, but sailing in the beautiful Caribbean was the ultimate. We were hooked to say the least. As our special week came to an end, we sure hated the thought of leaving Cancun and going back home to Michigan where everything was white and freezing.

14

Shock of a Lifetime

Six weeks after we returned from our lovely vacation my husband passed away suddenly. I was forty-nine years old at the time, and he had only been fifty-one years old. He had been retired for only eleven months from General Motors, and I was working for an orthodontist at the time as a receptionist/insurance biller. I had been working in the field for the past twenty years, but about a year after my husband died, the practice I had been working for was sold to a management company, and suddenly, people became numbers. With the stress of losing my husband and the stress of all the changes at work, I decided to quit. I gave the doctor my two weeks' notice and placed an AD in the local newspaper for house cleaning, and I prayed. From that one AD, my business grew and grew. Soon I was turning people down.

With the loss of my husband, I refocused on the other love of my life: horses. I have owned horses on and off for my entire life. After the loss of my husband, I bought another horse. My life consisted of cleaning houses, riding my horse, and spending a lot of time with my horsey friends, my family, and healing. It took me four years to feel the urge to take a vacation again. My daughter and I wanted to return to Cancun, and two of Laurel's girlfriends and coworkers wanted to go with us too. In February of 2000, we packed our bags once again and headed for Cancun. This time, believe me, we had passports instead of all those papers to keep in order. Of course, we had a wonderful time, even better than the first trip. I started to realize that I was not the one that had died and became alive again, laughing, singing, dancing, and celebrating life.

Vacations and Angels

When we went down for the second time, we stayed at the same hotel that we had stayed at the first time down there. We also wanted to go out on the same trimaran that we had gone out on the first trip down to Cancun. We went to the beach and to the marina that we thought we had gone to the first time and all bought tickets for the island tour. After we had purchased the tickets, we found out that it was not the same boat as before; we were actually going to be going out on a catamaran. We almost got our money back, but the salesperson convinced us that we would have a great time and would love the trip. So we went out on the catamaran, and the captain's name was Palemon. Palemon ended up being a big part in our lives in the up-and-coming years. We went out for the day on his boat and were very impressed with his sailing skills, his way of dealing with the tourists, and his character. We had a wonderful time once again and knew that we would be back again some day.

In April of 2000, we were on our way back to Cancun. On this trip, we spent almost every day out on the boats, sailing and snorkeling. We just could not get enough of the Caribbean atmosphere, the Mexican culture and people, everything! One of the days that we did not go out on a boat, I went by myself back to the marina where we had gone out with Palemon. I waited around until I spotted Palemon because I wanted to talk to him about Laurel and I meeting him later to talk about the boat business down there. When I left with a time to come back and meet, I did all I could do to remember his name. I kept saying to myself, "Pal o' mine," all the way on the bus back to the hotel until

I could write it down. Whew! We met that evening when he got through with work, and we sat and talked for a couple of hours to answer all the questions we could think of. I learned quite a lot, but I still needed clarification if I was to grasp the challenge that lay ahead. We paid him for his time and took him out to eat. We let him pick the place, and he led us to a very inexpensive and very good restaurant in Mercado 28 where I had ceviche mixto for the first time. The little suction cups on the side of the glass from the octopus grossed Laurel out, but the Mexican waiters snickering in the kitchen found this very amusing. We parted our ways with Palemon heading to Walmart to buy his son a birthday gift with the five hundred pesos we had given him. He came out a little later with one of those robot toys and a big smile. You've gotta get a little, warm, fuzzy spot for someone like that, someone who delighted in the small things in life, which made a difference for others. Before we knew it, the week was gone, and we were on our way back to Michigan again.

In February 2001, we were heading down to Cancun again; this time with Laurel's two children, Brittnay and Trenton, and my daughter-in-law, Lisa. My son, Mick, did not care to come along with us, but his wife Lisa wanted and was able to join us. She also fell in love with Cancun and the Caribbean and was just as happy as we were to be there. We did some special tours with the kids while we had them down there, and of course, we went out sailing and snorkeling. At first, Trenton was scared to death and was white as a ghost. One of the workers on the boat, Enrique, took Trenton in hand and started talking to him. Then he had Trenton up on his feet and was walking him all around the boat from front to back and side to side. He held Trent's hand the entire time and spent a lot of special time with him. By the end of the day, Trenton was like one of the mates on the boat. He got to swim with a shark, see sea turtles, and snorkel and got a lot of attention on the boat from the guys that were working as mates, especially from Enrique. As it turned out, Enrique and

Laurel became very good friends. Remember that this was our fourth time down to Cancun. Every time that we had been down there, we would go out on either a trimaran or catamaran, sailing and snorkeling for the day. This was our favorite thing to do down there. In previous years, I used to sail with my brother-in-law, Tom. He first started sailing on a day sailor and then he bought a twenty-seven-footer. After I started working, I met a woman named Paty who also liked to sail. In fact, she and her sister, Sandy, owned a twenty-five-foot sailboat. We became friends, and I started sailing with them. Before we knew it, we got into racing. We were the first all-women boat to race against the guys in the Saginaw Bay area. This was in the seventies, and the name of the boat was ERA (pronounced as *aira*). When we were not racing, we would go out for fun. On those times, I would sometimes take Laurel with us, and she also developed a love for sailing. Therefore, we were in heaven, sailing in the absolutely beautiful Caribbean. As it were, we were starting to be remembered and had friends by this time. We started talking to people and asking questions about the boat business in general.

1ˢᵗ Pic Please- Feburary 2001, When we went down for vacation. Left to Right: Daughter-in-law, Lisa, Laurel, Ruth, Trenton and Brittnay.

In May of 2001, I went down for ten days alone. In June, Laurel went down with friends and coworkers. By this time, Laurel had gone through a divorce. We started talking and dreaming and wishing to move down to Cancun. First, it was sort of joking, and then we really weren't joking any longer. We both bought books, such as *Spanish Made Simple*, and started trying to learn Spanish. We already had several CDs of Spanish music. The summer of 2001 was spent by us getting together every weekend either at my house or me hauling my dogs and sometimes my horse also to Laurel's house. Laurel lived on the west side of Michigan, and I lived on the east side. We would either be sitting out on my deck, talking of moving, listening to our favorite Hispanic group, Maná drinking Coronas or margaritas, and dreaming or doing the same in Laurel's backyard. Of course, the kids were there with us throughout our time of insanity. We all learned the words to our favorite song sung by Maná called "Reyondo El Sol." We would all sit around, singing this song all in Spanish even though we did not speak much Spanish at the time. Amazing! My grandchildren's ages at this time were fourteen years old, Brittnay, and ten years old, Trenton. I kept telling them that they needed to study Spanish with us, but both of them refused profusely to learn any Spanish.

Getting Serious

In September 2001, Laurel and I were on our way to Cancun again. This time, we had an appointment with a real estate agent. All of the people that we had been questioning and talking to about going into the boat business were very adamant about telling us *not* to get into the boat business. Everyone told us it is the most difficult business to get into. Therefore, we tried to heed everyone's advice and decided to look for something that we could turn into a bed-and-breakfast; there were none down there at that time. A bed-and-breakfast was something Laurel had always thought that she might like to do. Although the sailboat tour business was our passion, we were willing to do just about anything that we could to make a living down there.

We met with the owner/salesman almost as soon as we got off the plane once we found his office. All of these little signs of difficulty should have been little red lights going off in our brains, but we were too filled with the passion of wanting to live in Cancun to heed them. We had already decided that we would not be able to afford anything in Cancun, so we headed for Puerto Morelas, which is about twenty minutes south of Cancun. We spent three days with the realtor, looking, discussing, hoping, planning, and finally deciding we definitely could not afford to do this idea. He and his ex-wife/partner suggested that we just move down and work and live there for at least a year before doing anything. Needless to say, we did not heed this advice either. On Thursday morning, we were quite depressed and decided to go out on Palemon's catamaran for the day to cheer up. Yes, how can depression last when you are out sailing on that beautifully colored water with the sun shinning, the wind blowing through your hair, and a beautiful brown-skinned guy with a gorgeous smile waiting on you hand and foot. Not going to happen! While we were out there in "Palemon's big swimming pool," as he used to refer to the big sea green area out in front of the hotels where it is fun to stop and swim; we decided that this was exactly what we wanted to be able to offer people and what we wanted to do. We spent time after the tour talking and questioning Palemon once again. We flew back to Michigan on September 8, 2001. Three days later was September 11, 2001! How tragic and what a time to be thinking of starting a business out of the country. Another one of those flashing red lights we ignored.

We eventually decided to go on with the thought process of starting our own business of a sailing and snorkeling tour. I was getting very tired of living in limbo, constantly saying, "If we move to Cancun."

The next big step was to try to get permission through the court system to take Brittnay and Trenton out of the country and be able to move to Mexico. Their "father," I use the term loosely, would not give his written permission for the children to leave. Even though he was not a contributing factor in their well-being, Laurel still needed his permission. Laurel searched for an attorney that would take her case, and she was turned down several times (Another red light?). She finally found an attorney that listened to her plight; he told her he did not know if he could help nor how much it would cost, but he would try.

Her court date was set for November 19, 2001. We had both been very concerned about whether moving to Cancun and starting a business was going to be the absolute right thing to do. I am sure most of you cannot even begin to imagine what it would be like to just pull up roots and not only move but leave the country, and we were, of course, concerned about what it could do to the children. Neither one of them were the kind of student that excels in school, not that they were not intelligent; they just did not apply themselves to their full potential. To add to that, neither one of them wanted to move to Mexico. I think they probably were thinking like most of our friends and family were thinking, and that is that we would never pull it off. Unbeknown to Laurel, I began praying to God that if we were not going to be okay and if this was something that we should not be doing, please don't let us get permission from the court. If we were going to be okay, let the judge say yes. Laurel and I were talking on the phone, something we did every day; I told her what I had been praying. She said, "Mom, I have been praying for the same thing!" So we prayed this same prayer every day until November 19. We put the decision in God's hands. And this, my friends, is what we based the whole decision of to move or not to move. On November 19, 2001, I took off from work and drove over to Grand Rapids to go with Laurel to court. The fateful day was upon us, and we were both very nervous. You think? We found the courthouse, found a parking spot, and said a final prayer. We entered the building and found her attorney waiting for us, and as we entered the courtroom, another case was going on. We had to sit through that case and try to contain ourselves. Finally, it was Laurel's turn. She and her attorney settled themselves up front while I sat back by myself fidgeting. The judge came in, sat down, and looked over Laurel's case, and he then asked the attorney some questions. It didn't seem like the judge and the attorney had spoken to each other for more than a minute, and the judge did not ask Laurel one question. He announced, "If you want to move to Mexico, move, and if the children's father wants to see his children, he can move next door." At this point in time, the father was around $10,000 behind in child support. It happened so fast; I personally spoke up and asked the judge, "Does that mean we can move to Mexico?" He said yes. We had to hang around the courthouse until she got her legal documents, and then we were out of there. We got in the car and just started screaming, laughing, and doing high fives. I said to Laurel, "God knows we are so doubtful. He had to make it so simple that even we would know it was going to be okay." Now we had to tell the kids that we were going to go for it. When Laurel told Brittnay, she cried a lot and refused to talk to Laurel for a couple of weeks. Trenton was not too happy either.

Starting the Company

O kay, we are mentally ready to go ahead with everything, so what comes next? We needed to find an attorney, of course. How in the world do you find an honest and good attorney in a foreign country when you know absolutely nothing about any of the law firms in Cancun, we were thinking. Laurel started searching on line since she was the computer person and had a computer in her home. I had used them on my previous job for appointments, accounting, etcetera, but I used to grab my head a lot and fret! So Laurel started searching. She found one firm down in Cancun who had an affiliate office in Georgia. The firm in Cancun had an e-mail address, so she e-mailed them, telling them what we had in mind. The owner of the firm e-mailed her back with information, and they did this back and forth. I talked to him a couple of times on the phone, and we set up an appointment on January 2, 2002. Wow, we are actually going to do this thing, and we were both very excited and pensive at the same time. Laurel had lived in the Grand Rapids area for the past twelve years. She had basically raised her two children on her own. While she was working and trying to raise two children, she also managed to go to college for three years. She had worked at many jobs. She had been a waitress in a restaurant and worked her way up to a manager's position. She worked in a factory, and then she started working for one of the big banking corporations in Grand Rapids. She started as a teller and worked her way up the chain to the home equity department and was selling home equity lines of credit. We had to come up with a lot of money to start everything, and at first, I thought of selling my house and using the money to buy a boat and fund the business. The more I thought about this, the more I felt that I should not sell. One day, I called Laurel at work and told her that I did not think that I should sell my house. I said, "What if we do not make it down there and we have to come back, we will be out of money and have no place to live?" Therefore, I took out a home equity line of credit on my house and decided to rent it out while I was gone. We needed to have some security, and I also needed to pay the loan back; therefore, a renter was needed. Laurel worked with a great group of people, and she had two great bosses. They not only taught her a great deal, but they also cared for the people under them. We were trying to think of a name for our Mexican company. Laurel's head boss, Sam, came up with the idea of Too Much Fun-N-A Boat. When Laurel called me with this idea, I said, "Yes, and the *too* could be *two* for the two of us." That is how we arrived at a name for our company.

The four of us had our last Christmas together in my house. How very strange it seemed that this was to be our last Christmas in Michigan. God even blessed us with snow. Trenton received mostly things that he would be able to use in Mexico such as a new bike, roller blades, skateboard, and a soccer ball. I bought Brittnay a guitar because she had said that she would like to learn to play a guitar, and she had a beautiful singing voice and sang in the choir at school. I thought what better place to learn to play than in Mexico. She, at that time, wanted to be a singer and songwriter. Her idols at the time were the Backstreet Boys. She knew everything there was to know about all of them, and of course, she had her favorite. It was a wonderful Christmas and New Year.

Laurel and I were off for Cancun on January 2, 2002. We had fifteen days scheduled there to start the company and get things rolling. While we were there, we also needed to check out the American-accredited schools. Laurel had several schools to check from a list that she had obtained from her research on the Internet. The American-accredited schools were also set up and approved through the States, so if the kids wanted to go to a university in the

United States, they would have all their courses completed in high school. They would not have to take any additional college courses to catch up. These schools are duly certified, and after graduation, the kids may go to any college in the United States or in Mexico. They are quite expensive, costing from $350 to $600 a month per child plus an enrollment fee equal to one month's fee. In addition, books and supplies run anywhere from $200 to $400 (all prices are in US dollars). The public schools in Mexico only cost an enrollment fee of $30, which also includes insurance on the children in case of an accident while on school property. Once a child graduates from a public school, they may be accepted to a private Mexican university if they had good grades in high school. The public universities in Mexico are free and are only for the children that went to public schools and are from low income families. We heard that there is one university, the best in Mexico, for doctors and attorneys, which is in Mexico City, and it is a public university. The cost to go is an enrollment fee of $100 for the entire time a student is there including all books and supplies.

We had an appointment scheduled with our attorney about two hours after arrival time, thinking that this would be plenty of time. As it turned out, we barely had enough time to get to the appointment. It takes awhile to get through customs and get transportation to downtown. We were no longer staying in the expensive hotel zone; we had a room reserved downtown as we just had time to check in, get rid of our luggage, and get to the attorney's office. As it turned out, the hotel and the office were within half a mile from each other, so we could walk and not have to pay for a taxi. We didn't even have time to change from our shorts to our business clothes. We made it on time and met the Señor for the first time in person. It turned out to be a very nice office, very professional. We sat down and explained what we wanted, and he listened. He then explained some things to us, one being that we had to have a Mexican partner. Because the particular business we had chosen was in the Mexican waters, we had to have a Mexican partner that would "own" 51 percent of our business. After talking with us for probably an hour,

our attorney wanted to talk to me alone without Laurel present. When he got me off by myself, he tried to tell me how difficult this was going to be. He tried to call a friend of his who owned a similar business on Cozumel because he wanted me to talk to him. He also gave one of his assistants the job of making a list of everything that we would need in order to be able to get up and running. He told me, "You get all of the answers to these questions and then come back and see me. If you still want to start your company, then we will do so." He wouldn't take any money from me until we came back with the answers.

The list first involved going to the harbor master, also known as el capitania del puerto or captain of the port. Each port has one of these official offices. They control everything that has to do with anything on the Mexican waters. They are the god of the waters, as we used to refer to them. There is an office in Puerto Juarez, on Isla Mujeres, Puerto Morelos, and so on. Of course, no one in these offices speak English. Number two, find a place to dock the boat once it was there. Number three, find someone to deliver the boat.

Laurel had a friend whom she had met in February 2001 when we were down with the kids. His name is Enrique, and we met up with him after our first meeting with our attorney. I also had a friend, Miguel, whom I had met in February 2000. The four of us rented a car the next day to go out to Puerto Juarez to the harbor master's office to get a list of all the permits that we would need to be able to start the business. Before we were allowed to get into the car, the guys went totally around the car with the guy that was renting it out, and they made sure every little mark, dent, or scratch was marked on the sheet of paper. This was a good thing because when we returned the car, they tried to blame some damage on us. Luckily, we had someone with us to argue that point! When we got to the harbor master's office, of course, no one spoke English, so Enrique did our talking for us. It was explained that we would need to acquire seven permits all in a sequence and that they were all available. We inquired about snorkeling permits as well, and we were told that those were available also. However, none of these permits can be applied for until we had the boat there. Okay, we thought, that all sounded simple enough as we walked out. We then drove up the coast toward Punta Sam, looking for a place to dock the boat. We did not look in the hotel zone for dockage because we assumed we could not afford it. We found one place that we thought might work. It needed a bit of work on the land around the dock and the dock itself, so we drove further up the coast. We found what we thought was *the* perfect place! It was a restaurant in Punta Sam, called The Pelican. It had indoor and outdoor dining; it was quiet and rather a classy place with a beautiful, almost new dock and no boats docked at it. When we walked in, we could go to the left and be in the restaurant or walk straight and go out to the beach. There was a wooden walkway with a vine-covered trellis out to the beach where there were palm trees blowing in the breeze. This place was exactly what I had pictured in my dreams. We were so excited, especially me. I could not have come closer to what I had pictured in my dreams if I had to draw it and build it myself!

Picture of the first place that we found to dock our boat
the week we were down to start the company.

You see, Laurel had dreams of working on the boat, and my dreams were to be on the beach in a little palapa, selling tickets to the tourists. I could just picture myself and my rottweiler, Fargo, sitting around under the palm trees in the cool white sand, listening to Mexican music, talking to people, selling lots of tickets, and living the dream life. We checked out the whole place and then went searching for the owner. We found him in the restaurant, and he was not too friendly. He was an older gentleman who was originally from Spain. The Spaniards who have gone to Mexico to live see themselves above the Mexican people in general. They are a very proud and of the old-world race more times than not. He spoke to Enrique, not even giving Laurel nor I a glance. Enrique explained what we intended to do. We discussed things with him as we walked out to the beach, and he even gave me permission to have a palapa built on his beach under some palm trees. He also said that I could bring my dog with me. We agreed on a price, and we told him we would return in a few days with a contract. Wow! Things were coming together. On the way back to Cancun, we stopped to have some ceviche and some cervezas (of course). While we were eating, Enrique asked the owner/waiter if he knew any captains that deliver boats from the United States. Actually, he did, and he told Enrique about the guy. As we left the restaurant and were walking down the road to our car, this guy came up behind us in a jeep. He stopped and talked to us, and it turned out that he was the captain that delivered boats! We talked to him about delivering the kind of boat we had in mind to buy, and he said he had no problem with such a job. Okay! We had the list, the dock, and a guy to deliver the boat all in one day! We were on our way! We called the attorney's office and set up another appointment to start the company.

We met the next day and explained that we were sure and ready to begin, so they drew up everything that we needed to proceed. We had asked Enrique to be our Mexican partner, and he said that he would. When all the papers are drawn up, there is a way that they (attorneys and the law) cover the American investor so that you are not risking your company. We were informed that we had to find an accountant and also had to decide on how we were going to split the stock. We had three or four more meetings at the attorney's office. The whole process ran down to the last night before we were booked to leave. We had last-minute meetings with the accountant's office and the attorney and the notario. A notario is similar to an attorney, we found out. We had no clue, but they draw up a lot of the legal documents such as rental agreements, and for us, they made three books. We were given these books the last night before we left. One was our acta. An acta is all the rules and bylaws of the company. The acta explains exactly what the company will be doing, what kind of product it will be producing, and in our case, what we could claim as a business expense. All three books were explained as they were written in Spanish, but we never did quite understand what exactly they were for or what we were supposed to do with them. We did, however, guard them with our lives, so to speak, and have them to this day. On our last day in Cancun, we had to run to the accountant's office for some very important documents, which had to be signed and also be delivered to the attorney's office. Luckily, offices in Mexico are open until 8:00 or 9:00 p.m. Whew! We made it. We finished around 10:00 p.m., and the next morning, we flew out. However, the accountant needed my passport for more documents. Once I got back home to the states, I had to send, through FedEx, my passport back to the accountant's office. She did what she needed to do and then sent it back to me through FedEx.

An Angel Appears

A round the beginning of the year 2000, Laurel was on the computer, looking for a place to go scuba diving in or around Cancun. She was in a chat room and met a guy by the name of Scuba Kevin. She talked to him about diving, and he happened to be living in Cancun. He was managing a dive shop down there, and they chatted back and forth occasionally for about a year. Suddenly, he just dropped out of the picture. Shortly after we had started our company, he coincidentally popped in online. She told him everything that we had been doing, and he suddenly became our first and biggest angel in our future life. He told her approximately what it should cost per month to live in Cancun. Laurel and Kevin had been talking for quite a few months. He had helped us out with so much already. The first time that Laurel told him we had started a business, his first question was, "Oh, what does your business plan look like?" It took her a minute to answer because she had no idea what a business plan was. She tried explaining to him that we certainly didn't need a business plan because this was just going to be a simple thing between her and me. All we wanted to do was get down there and maybe hand out information on the beach or the buses. I was going to sit under a palapa on the beach in front of our boat, and we were sure the people were just going to come up to us and ask to go out on our boat! That was our business plan! Kevin proceeded to give Laurel her first lesson on having a business! She thinks it was right then that he thought if he didn't help, we weren't going to have a chance down there, and he walked her through quite a bit online. Laurel was a single mom at that time, and after her kids went to bed, the Internet was how she entertained herself. She would be on the computer for hours at a time, and thank God, that is how she met Kevin to begin with.

When we went down in March, we got to meet Kevin in person. We met him one evening at a restaurant and had dinner. I actually wore a dress, and Laurel had on a skirt and blouse. It was probably the only time we ever wore a dress or skirt the whole entire time we lived there except when we went to a wedding! We were trying to look professional. We were informed by Kevin that most businesses down there were done with dressing casually. Oh, well, what did we know? He was very informative and quite concerned for both of us to say the least. When we left him, we had plans to meet again when we went down in May.

Kevin was married, and his wife's name is Hanna. Kevin is an American, and Hanna is Mexican. They moved to Cancun from New Jersey. Kevin's business back in the states, we found out, was as a consultant to businesses that were failing. A company that was in trouble would call him to come in and fix their business so they could make money again. How cool was that to meet someone with his business knowledge? When we met him, he and his wife had been living in Cancun for about ten years. By the time we met him in person, he had his own business and still does. He does graphic design, websites, some small business consulting, web hosting, and photography of which he has a database right now of eighteen thousand photos of Mexico, but his principal activity is design and programming of websites. He is very good and designed our website for us as well. Since he had his own business and was working out of his house at that time, he was his own boss. He was fluent in Spanish, having learned it from working on the dive boats. He said every day he would have class with the guys for about an hour. Kevin also knew a lot of people down there that were influential business owners, and he and Hanna had once both worked at the Royal Resorts.

Kevin decided to take us under his wing; he had wings because he was an angel, remember?, and all we can say is that God must have whispered in his ear. That is the only way we have of explaining all that he and Hanna did for us in the time that we were down there not to mention Hanna's sister Elvia and Elvia's husband, Raul.

Laurel and I had to make a sudden trip down to Cancun in March. We went for a total of three days. Our attorney was concerned that they had not received our RFC delivered to their office by our partner, Enrique, nor could they get in touch with him. So we had to jump on a plane to go down and find out what was going on with Enrique. This was an expense that neither one of us could afford, but it was a definite necessity. We arrived and checked in to our hotel, the same one that we had been using for a while now. To our surprise and delight, Enrique met us there and couldn't, for the life of him, understand why we were so upset with him. It turned out that he actually had our RFC—this is a very important item that you need when you have a business down there. I am not going to try to explain what all the documents that we had to get were for because I do not think that many would be interested in why, just how many we actually had to get, and the trouble it was to get them. We took the RFC to the attorney's office with the official papers that came with it. At this time, we were thinking that we probably would have to find a more responsible person to be our Mexican partner.

We also took one whole day in our three days and rented a little, and I mean little, boat. Because we wanted to go over to an island that Enrique had suggested to us for tours. The name of the island is Isla Contoy and is a bird sanctuary, which is protected by the government like our federal parks. We were heading over there in this little boat that we found to rent with a captain of sorts and his helper, and the further out we got, the bigger the waves. As the waves increased in size, the smaller the boat seemed. Enrique went with us, and as we left shore, he took the only life jacket in the boat and put it on himself. Survival of the fittest in its most perfect form. When we got to the island, the captain took us on a little tour around some of it and into the cove where all the birds live. There was a little fishing village on one end of the island, and then the rest was pretty much the sanctuary. There were snorkeling reefs over there, and when we landed, there was a very nice dock for our use to load and unload passengers. The beach is absolutely beautiful, very peaceful, and undisturbed. We took several pictures and could sell them for postcards; they are all so magnificent. It would have been a great place for us to run a tour. It was something for us to keep in mind. We had met with Kevin twice in the three days, and on the third day, we were on our way home to Michigan once again.

Buying a Boat

B y this time also, Laurel had been searching for a boat online. We had in mind a McGregor 36 catamaran because that is the kind of boat Palemon had been sailing every time that we had gone out with him. We really liked the boat—the way it was built, the amount of people that you could get on it, and the price range was in our ball park. Laurel had found many other boats, trimarans, and cats, but they just did not look like they would hold enough people. She found one McGregor for sale in California. I called and talked to the owner about the boat. He sent more pictures. I then hired a boat surveyor that he recommended to me to do a boat survey. This guy did a good job for us, and in a couple of weeks, I had the survey in my hands. I then took it to my brother-in-law, whom I used to sail with, Tom. Tom had also done boat surveying in his lifetime and had a sailboat for many years. He also raced as a crew member on many of the big boats in the Sarnia to Mackinaw races and quite a few other races. He said according to the survey, the boat looked pretty good. Then we started investigating how to get it to Cancun from California. This particular boat can be taken apart and trailered. The big problem with that is we would have to be able to put it back together again once we would get it there! We thought about launching it in Corpus Christi, Texas, and sailing it from there to Cancun. I called the boat surveyor and asked him his advice. He suggested taking it apart, packing it in a shipping box, and either shipping it by ship or train. I had a friend that I used to ski with who worked for an import/export company. I called her up and asked her if she could find out for me how much it would cost to ship this boat over to Cancun. She told me, "You do not want to send it by train because it will probably never get there." So our option was to ship it by ship. She told me it would take her a couple of days to get an answer for me. A couple of days later, she called me with the approximate price of $20,000, plus we would have to pay an import tax once it arrived. It could take ten months to a year to get there, and someone would have to be there to take delivery. The price pretty much told us to forget this boat! Once again, Laurel started searching. She found one out in Massachusetts. From the pictures, it did not look too bad, and the price was certainly right. I asked my brother-in-law, Tom, who was retired, to fly out there with me to check out the boat. I bought his ticket and paid all his expenses. When we got there, it was very, very cold and windy. We took one whole day, rented a car, and drove out to where the boat was in dry dock. Tom took most of the day to check out the boat from top to bottom, side to side. It really was not in very good condition. I talked with the owner quite awhile, hemmed and hawed, trying to decide what to do. We discussed what options I had as far as getting it down the coast to Florida. As it turned out, they were getting ready to go down to Florida to a regatta. They discussed among themselves how they could get the boat down there for me. They were very nice; in fact, I contacted many boat people while doing all this, and everyone could not do enough for me. If you have a boat, are into sailing and racing, or whatever, you are like family, it seemed. As it turned out, I eventually decided this was not going to be the boat either. The end of March or very first days of April, Laurel found two McGregors in Florida. They were in a much better area; that is for sure. There was one in St. Petersburg and one in one of the most southern Keys, Big Pine Key. I checked with Tom to inquire as to whether he would be able to go with me down to Florida to check out these boats with me. He told me that he would be able to do so, and we flew out on April 7, 2002. We got to St. Pete at 6:50 p.m. I had a rental car reserved and also a hotel room via Laurel who had made the reservations online. We picked up the car and proceeded to find the hotel. We went out to dinner, and I had my first taste of coconut shrimp. *Yum.* The next morning, we got up early and found the boat marina. The owner of the boat,

Justin, was there to greet us, and Tom proceeded with his survey of the boat. It looked to be in pretty good condition. He spent two to three hours checking things over, and then we were on our way to the Keys. We arrived in the evening, and I called the owner of the other boat to set up an early appointment to go and see the other boat. He told me it would be about a forty-five-minute drive from where we had spent the night. Once again, the next day, we were up at the crack of dawn, driving south to check out the other boat. This one was a hard deck, which Laurel and I thought at the time might be good for the people to sit on, plus you could put the coolers on it with no problem. Well, I had pictured in my mind a fiberglass hard deck. When we got to the marina, the guy met us, and we had to take a little speedboat ride over to see the boat. It was shoved up into the mangroves, and we had to climb from the little boat onto the cat. I did not really like the looks of this boat right off the bat, but I couldn't let that stop me from buying the best one. This one did not have a motor; I would have to buy one first thing. It was rigged with steel piping with a canopy over the hard deck. This also would have been a nice feature for when our tourists were out and it was really hot and sunny. However, the hard deck was made out of plywood. I could just picture these sweet young things sliding their you-know-what across that plywood in a string bikini. Ouch! The guy that owned it was a bit unusual to say the least. I had all these things running through my mind. We finally were ready to leave the boat. We took our little trip back across as I was talking to the owner about buying a new motor and how we were going to get it on the boat and such things as that. Tom and I thanked him and went on our way toward the north. We stopped for breakfast, and we discussed the boats. He was very impartial, just telling me the good and bad about both boats. He was very careful about letting me make up my own mind. I called Laurel from the restaurant and told her that we were going to own a boat when I left Florida. I just didn't know which one. I described both of them to her and asked which one she would choose. She said, "Mom, you are there seeing them. I am not. It would be better if you decide for us." So I did! I decided on the one in St. Pete. We drove back up to St. Pete, and by the time we got there, it was evening. I called Justin, the owner, and told him that I had decided on his boat. We met early the next morning. I had, as I have said earlier, taken out a home equity line of credit on my home to finance some of the business. I had checks and a credit card issued from that account. I wrote Justin out a check for the boat, and we went to the bank to cash it. They would not clear the check immediately, which means that Justin could not sign over the title of the boat to me. I was flying out of there around 1:00 p.m. that day. I had the bank call the bank where the loan originated and where my daughter was working at that time. She talked to the people at the Florida bank on the phone; she had her boss talk to them also. It was no good. Justin, unfortunately, did not have a "home" bank in St. Pete. I guess he did not believe in them; I don't remember the particulars. He did, however, have a friend who was a bank manager at another bank. We then went to that bank, and finally, the check was okayed, and we were able to clear everything up before I flew out. Whew! *Again!*

The day I bought the boat. Left-previous owner.
Right-Tom, my brother-in-law

Okay, we now are proud owners of a boat. We are living in Michigan, the boat is in Florida, and our company is in Mexico. Now comes the task of finding someone to deliver the boat to Cancun. There was no way for us to find or contact the captain that we had spoken to originally the day we were getting the list filled for the attorney. Laurel started contacting boat-moving companies in the United States. Everyone she contacted, and this ended up to be twelve or thirteen companies, would tell her, "Sure, we have no problem delivering your boat to Cancun. Send us the specs about the boat and a picture." She would do so, and they would all say that they could not move this particular boat as there would be no place to get out of a storm if there should be one on the way down to Cancun. Either they would say no or they would not even bother contacting her back.

In May, Laurel and I both went down to get some things finalized for the business. We also needed to find a house to rent. We took Trenton down with us this time and left Brittnay back in the States. She stayed with one of her girlfriends so that she could continue to go to school. She was in the ninth grade by this time. Trenton was able to bring his schoolwork with him. We stayed in the hotel zone and rented a condo. It was actually cheaper for us than just a room as we could cook, and it had a refrigerator to store food and drinks. We did this so that Trent could play in the Caribbean and the pool and not be stuck downtown with nothing much to do. We got newspaper ads and looked for houses. We had our friends look at where these places were (good or bad) for us to live, and then Enrique would call for us. We viewed several places, mostly apartments, but I just could not picture myself living in any of them. One day, Laurel and I were taking a walk around the attorney's office in that area, and there was this car that was broken down, sitting in the street. We walked by it, and I noticed a sign in the window for a house for rent. As it turned out, it was in a good area of Cancun, and the rent was reasonable (we thought). When we called, the owner spoke English. She met us and showed us the house. It was in a very nice neighborhood with lots of trees and a park one house down from the rental house. This would be perfect for both Trenton and Fargo, my Rottweiler. The house had a living room, dining area, kitchen, two bedrooms upstairs, and a bathroom both upstairs and downstairs. We decided to take it. Then we had to go to a notario and have a contract drawn up. We, of course, had to pay for this. We went and met the owner there and had the papers drawn up. Needless to say, by this time, you are probably guessing, the papers were not ready until the last day that we were there. Boy oh boy, things are always a close call down there. When we left, we had a house to move into once we arrived with all our stuff. Yeah! While we were down there, we also looked up Palemon and told him that we had started our company, had bought the boat, and were moving down in June of 2002. We wanted him to come and be our captain. We had already drawn up a sort of work contract for him showing what we were willing to offer. This is one of the things that Laurel and I had decided right from the beginning. We were going to pay our employees a fair wage and treat them fairly also. What we offered Palemon was almost twice as much as he was making at that time, having worked for that particular company for twelve years. He would not say that he would come and work for us. He said that he was too afraid that us being women and new at the business, he did not think that we would make it. He said that he had two children and a wife to feed and could not take the chance. We told him, "Okay, if you change your mind, let us know."

Toward the end of May and into June, Laurel went down by herself because one of us needed their FM3 to be able to bring all our belongings across the border. When she found out one of us had to have a visa (FM3) to bring our belongings across the boarder, it was just logical that she went. She had been working for a bank for several years. In January 2002, when we returned from Cancun after starting our business, she found out that the bank had been bought out. She also found out that her department was being transferred to Cincinnati, Ohio, and she was going to be without a job in April. This to her felt like another sign that we were doing the right thing. She was unemployed, and I was still cleaning houses. After talking with Kevin, he checked into what she would have to do to get her visa. He figured that they could get it done in seven days, so she booked her flight for ten days just to be sure. She arrived there in the early afternoon and went right to the house we had previously rented. It was completely empty, so the first thing she did was go shopping for a hammock and some food that she could keep out on the counter. She also bought cleaning supplies as the house had been empty for a while and was a little dirty. She cleaned all that day and hung the hammock and went to sleep early. She had no lights because for some reason, the electricity wasn't working. The first full day she met Kevin, and they went to immigration with the paperwork and handed it in. After having to run to the internet or copy shop around the corner to correct a couple of documents that were not correct and standing in line, they probably got out of there in four hours after arriving. All of the documents that you hand into the immigration office have to be originals and have two copies included with them. She had to have the application, her passport with two copies of every page (even the blank pages), the business acta, a list of employees, a bill from our house that we were renting, the RFC, and a letter from the company explaining her employment in the company. She handed all these in and received a date to come back in three days and check on the documents. She used those three days and shopped for a refrigerator and a bed. She found both and had them delivered to the house. After getting the refrigerator, she went out and bought some food to last the rest of the days that she would be there. She also bought a tank of gas (propane is what all the stoves in Mexico are run on). They sell tanks off a truck that comes around the neighborhood every day. It was fifteen US dollars for gas, and there was an empty tank out back, so she did not have to actually buy the tank, just a refill. She had to buy a pan for cooking and some utensils but didn't buy much because she knew we were bringing everything down when we moved. She didn't have a TV, so she did a lot of reading. She also had a very nice neighbor come over and help her with the electricity. It seems the fuse box had just been turned off. She had taken her CD player down on the plane with her, so she had music; and when she left Cancun, she left them at the house. She bought a broom and some bathroom supplies and really enjoyed setting up house while she was there, but it did get a little lonely. On the third day, Kevin and Laurel went back to immigration, and her visa was not ready. They wanted some more documentation and were questioning whether she had the authority to sign the letters from the company. Kevin had to show them her powers of the company in the acta, and then the immigration office had to resubmit the new documentation and corrections and set up a new appointment time in two days. She was coming close to the end of her stay and hadn't received her visa and was getting a little stressed at that point. It didn't seem to be running as smoothly as Kevin thought it would, and she had only six days left. They told Kevin, "Don't worry. It should be done in two days." They went back in two days, and it still was not ready because they were questioning something new. They had to get additional documents once again, and she told them that her flight was scheduled to leave in two days. They said this would be the last of the documents needed, but it would not be ready by the time she was supposed to leave. She went to Kevin's house and changed her flight for three days later than originally booked and then called me to let me know what was going on and prayed! She went back on the twelfth day and had to be interviewed by Salvador, who seemed to be one of the only nice people in the immigration office. It was quick and painless; he asked her what color her eyes were, how tall she was, why she wanted to be in Mexico, and that was it. She then had her visa! Whew! The worry was over! The next day she was on her way back to Grand Rapids with a house still to pack and seven days to do so.

While she was there getting her visa, Kevin was with her almost every day. They went to see a friend of his who worked in the only marina in Cancun, Hacienda del Mar. They asked if he knew of anyone that was qualified to bring a boat over from Florida. He gave them the names and phone numbers of three men. They called the first guy and set up a time to meet with him in what became our office, El Cafe. After about a twenty-minute interview, they had the price and information. When the guy left, they both looked at each other and could read in each other's faces the feelings. They were on the same page and did not feel comfortable with that guy. The next phone number was disconnected. The third number put them in contact with Carlos Austin, who is the owner of a small marina on the canal side of Cancun called Mundo Marina. He offers dive trips and deep sea fishing, and he also owns the restaurant next door to the marina now known as Captain Charlies. They called and set up a time to meet him at the marina, and after about forty minutes of talking with Carlos, she signed a contract to hire him right there on the spot. No one in the United States had the courage to bring our boat over for us, but Carlos had no problem with sailing our boat over for us. He has been delivering boats back and forth, to and from Cancun and to the United States and back for twenty-five years or more. He just felt like family immediately to her. Her instincts turned out to be correct, and he became another angel in our lives and a wonderful friend to us both until today.

Most of the houses down there have hammock hooks in the walls in the living room and also the bedrooms. They were also outside in the back in our little cemented wall in the back area. That is where we would put a washing machine. There were also hooks for clotheslines. In the front of the house, the yard was gravel. It was all fenced in, and there was a place to park one small car within the fenced area. There was a big palm tree that grew within the fenced area and some little ones as well. Out in the street, there were a lot of trees along the sidewalk. It was very shaded and a very nice neighborhood. It was a good place for us to begin.

The 1st house that Laurel and I rented
together. Trenton is inside the gate.

Kevin and Hanna were so worried about us driving down
through Mexico. They were sure we were going to get robbed or
killed or both as were our friends and family. Kevin insisted on
giving Laurel one of their cell phones, which we could use once
we crossed the border. That way, he could keep track of us, and we
could call him if we needed help with anything. She was given
his cell phone number and also Hanna's. All of this concern from
people whom we had just met for only two times in our lives!

Laurel returned to the United States, and now we had to get
serious about getting our life here in the States in order. Both
of our vehicles had to be paid for because you cannot take your
vehicle across the border without a clear title. We had to try to
decide what we could take and what we couldn't. Fortunately for
me, there was one of my girlfriends, who was also into horses,
who was interested in renting my house. I did not know her very
well, but I felt I could trust her to take very good care of my
house and yard. She is a police officer and a single woman, so my

house would not be trashed by children. As it turned out, it was an excellent decision. I have an acre of lawn to be cut and lots of trees with falling branches all the time or leaves in the fall. She did an excellent job of caring for my place, and she also allowed me to store some of my bedroom furniture and other things that I could not take yet wanted to keep stored in one of the empty bedrooms. Thank you, Beth! I originally had plans of coming up the next year, getting my horse and packing the rest of the things that I had left behind in the horse trailer and hauling it all down.

Meeting the Mexican Consulate

Laurel and I had to compose a list of every single item that we were taking right down to salt and pepper shakers. We then had to have that list translated into Spanish. I had just taken a short Spanish class through our local college, and my instructor was a licensed translator. He was called upon to translate for various things such as in court for instance. He translated the list from English to Spanish. It ended up being a ten-paged, double-spaced typed list! It cost me $110 to have it translated. We then had to take this list down to Detroit, Michigan, to the Mexican consulate to be approved. That was a treat, let me tell you. We drove down one day and took the kids with us. We finally found the place and found a parking lot, which ended up costing us $22 to park for about an hour—two at the most! We went in, and as I recall, we were the only ones there that were not Mexican. It was very intimidating to say the least. However, this was something that we were going to have to get used to real quick. After waiting awhile, we were ushered into the head office. The guy checked over our list; actually, he just glanced at it, charged us $137 cash, of course, and then had to stamp every page with his official stamp that said approved. We were on our way. It was our first lesson in pay off or bribe or whatever you want to call it. They called it a fee.

Finalization

L aurel had to obtain all of the kids' school records, all our birth certificates, my dog's heath certificate from my veterinarian and take all these records down to Lansing, our state capitol, to have them apostled. This is a gold seal that the state puts on each document. I had to set up a separate bank account so that the renter could put her rental money into this account, and then my house payment could be automatically taken out of that account to pay my home equity loan that I had taken out. I also had to open an account for my horse so that her board money could be taken out as well as money for the blacksmith, veterinarian, or whatever she might need while I was gone. I then had to start dealing with my house and packing, and just trying to decide where to begin was overwhelming. Every box that we packed had to be marked on the flap or somewhere on the box what was inside for immigration at the border. I was taking my kitchen table and four chairs, a lazy boy and glider chair, my entertainment center torn apart of course, and TV. That was all my big stuff. Everything that we took that had a model number on it had to be listed with the name of the item on the list. Our departure date was set for June 16, 2002, and we would not be allowed to vary that date by much because we had made arrangements with Enrique to meet us at the border on a certain day. Laurel paid for his airplane ticket from Cancun to Matamoros, Mexico, and we had a date set to meet him at a certain hotel that we had reservations booked for the night. Enrique then would drive through Mexico with us to help with translations and try to keep us safe. I cannot explain exactly what it took or how you know how to get ready for a move like this; we just did it. I guess this is as good a place as any to try to explain how we started to inform our friends and family of our decision. My son was the second to the last that I told. I guess because I knew that it would be so difficult to explain the reason for our decision to move and knowing that I would not be seeing him, my four-year-old grandson, my twelve-year-old step-granddaughter and daughter-in-law. Laurel and I planned a cookout so that we could break the news together with them. I first told my daughter-in-law, Lisa, and got her reaction. I then told my son, Mick, and he actually took the news very well and told me that he only wanted my happiness. Laurel and I were both very relieved when they accepted the news with much grace and encouragement. The next person I then had to tell was my sister, Dale. I dreaded this more than almost anything, but I had to buck up and do it. She is twelve years older than me and has always been kind of a second mother to me. I knew it would be very hard on her and hard for her to accept. She does not accept changes very well and is the type of person that likes routine and does not like to travel. I had a very difficult time trying to explain my wants and needs for this extreme move, and she never really understood nor accepted the fact that I moved away. She absolutely refused to ever call me or write to me, which hurt my feelings, but I understood that she was angry with me for moving. It wasn't easy for Laurel and I to try to explain the compelling feeling that we both had to do something like this, but it was there. It was either try or sit around the rest of our lives wondering what if. Once all our family and friends knew what we were planning on doing, we felt much better, and it was a relief not to have to keep this secret any longer. All of my friends and family were very concerned for us and very worried, not only for our well-being but worried that we would not be successful. No one really thought that we would be able to accomplish everything that was needed for us to be up and running as a tour. My sister was sure that I would be back within a year; after all, what do two women from the United States know about starting a boat business in Mexico. We knew absolutely nothing, and when you hear ignorance is bliss, in this case, it certainly was. What chance did we have, never having owned a boat before, never owning a business before nor speaking Spanish? We felt that we had every chance in the world because we knew in our hears that God was with us all the way. He is the only way that I can explain how we were able to get as far as we did. It was God's will to allow us our will.

My 1996 Z71 Chevy Silverado pickup had to have some major work done on it before I could leave Michigan. I also had to get four new tires and also new tires for the trailer that I was going to be hauling. My husband had a little eight-foot wooden trailer that he used to haul his four-wheeler around with, and when he died, I had sold the four-wheeler but kept the trailer. I had to have the wiring redone on the trailer and a few other things repaired before the trip. I also had a camper top on the back of my pickup, and that was the entire packing space we had to incorporate two households of belongings to take with us. The rest had to go or be stored. On the last day that I spent in my home, I finished packing and loading the trailer and cleaning my house for the renter. When my son got out of work that day, he came down and helped me pack the heavy furniture, and I think it was around 6:00 p.m. when we finally finished packing. We then had to try and tie down a tarp covering everything in the trailer, and by then, it was raining! Another red flag? I hugged and kissed my son for the last time in quite a while and loaded my Rottweiler, Fargo, and I was on my way to begin the journey of a lifetime. I drove to Grand Rapids, three hours from my house, in the rain most of the way. By the time that I arrived, the tarp that we had so carefully tied down was flapping in the breeze! When I pulled up to Laurel's house, she looked out the window at how full the trailer looked, figured there would be no room for anything of hers, and started crying. I assured her when I got into the house that there would be room for everything that she planned on taking. The next day we got up early and started packing the remainder of her things that she had not gotten a chance to pack because of being delayed by the immigration department in Mexico.

We packed and cleaned and cleaned and packed and threw out a lot of belongings. I had thrown out quite a bit myself as I had not moved in thirty years. As we were trying to pack the trailer, we were just in the process of wondering how in the world we were going to get everything in especially Laurel's washing machine. She was also taking a dresser and a wooden bed with mattress and box springs along with the normal household items. We had already made a trip to Menards for a new and sturdier tarp and buckle straps, bungee cords, and rope. We were fretting about how we were going to get everything in while getting more and more tired by the minute, and who pulled up? My niece Chris and her husband Mike. I have two nieces and a nephew who are more like my children than nieces and nephew. They are my brother-in-law Tom's children, the same Tom who helped me find a boat. We are very close because Tom had gotten divorced when the children were very young, and while Tom was working during the summers, they stayed at my house during the days. We all spent a lot of time and holidays together, so we were all very close. My two children thought of them as sisters and brother. It was so special that Chris and Mike should show up like that and help us pack. We almost unpacked the whole trailer and started again. It was pack, unpack, move things, rearrange things, and rearrange them again. It took us all day and into the night, but we finally got-r-done. We ended up not covering the trailer because we figured that the tarp would just rip again. We were finally ready to pull out in the morning with Laurel driving her 1997 Cavalier with one of the kids riding with her, and I was, of course, driving my truck and pulling the trailer. The cab of my truck was jam-packed with things that could not fit anywhere else, plus my Rottweiler had the back with the seat flipped up for more room for him plus Brittnay in the passenger seat.

The trailer load that we packed in Mi.

Starting Our Big Trip

I am an early riser, especially when I have someplace to go or something to do. Laurel, on the other hand, likes to sleep in. We really had never discussed what time we planned on leaving. I just assumed it would be early. She, on the other hand, assumed it would be when she got up and started moving around and we got around to leaving. I woke her up at the crack of dawn, which did not go over too great with her. I thought, *Oh, oh, what a way to start our new life together and living together and owning a business together!* She got over it, and we were on our way. We did have to make a stop for gas, and we also stopped and bought two two-way radios with an approximate range of two miles. This was Laurel's idea, and it was a lifesaver to have them. We were first heading down to Arkansas to my brother's house. He had recently moved down there and had built his house himself at the ripe ole age of sixty-eight years! He had had enough of the Michigan winters and decided that he wanted to live in a warmer climate. We drove straight through the first day, basically stopping only for gas, food, or potty breaks for us and Fargo. On the second day, we did stop at Meremack Caverns in Arkansas to do a little sightseeing. What a beautiful place that is, and we were certainly glad that we had taken the time to see it. We had also tried to get a close-up look at the arch over the Mississippi River, but we could not find a way to get close because I was pulling the trailer and hadn't gotten used to backing it up yet. It was also so loaded that it was difficult to maneuver for me.

Left to Right: Brittany, Laurel, Ruth, Trenton and Fargo (dog)

We arrived at my brother's house around 5:00 p.m., just in time for dinner. When we drove into his driveway, I am sure he took one look at how we were packed and almost had heart failure. We looked like the Beverly Hillbillies, if you are old enough to remember that TV show. My brother, Keith, had been a manager of a moving van company for years, so his expertise was packing! He was up early the next morning, and when I walked out into his pole barn where he had me park my truck and trailer, he was already hard at work. We ended up spending almost the entire day unloading and reloading the trailer. He added a sheet of plywood up front standing on end so that it stood in the air approximately eight feet. He then added sheets of plywood to each side, and then we repacked again! Once the trailer was repacked to his liking, he then took the tarp and used bolts and screws and fixed it to the front piece of plywood. We then tied the tarp with rope and used bungee cords and also the heavy ratchet straps. Then when that was all finished, he mounted one bike on one wheel well and one bike on the other wheel well, removing the bike peddles on the inside close to the trailer so that they would ride sturdy without bouncing. He did an excellent job to say the least as he has a tendency toward perfection as I do. "If it is not done well, it is not worth doing" is a motto that we grew up with.

This is Laurel's view and version of our visit to Uncle Keith's house. When we arrived at Uncle Keith's house, I was so relieved to get a couple of days downtime. Ha! I about ran away when he suggested that we repack the trailer. I am not the most organized person, and I felt our packing job got us that far. Why change it? Then I figured, well, he will just move some things around, and then we can enjoy our day of visiting with Uncle Keith and Aunt Jo. When we got into his pole barn the next day and I realized what he wanted to do, I could have kicked myself for ever stopping! He wanted to unpack the whole trailer! The Dobson family sometimes look for work to do if they are bored and think hard work is always more fun than just sitting around visiting, my Mom included in that category. I had come to discover this fact when I was a kid! I did not want to have anything to do with this crazy idea of his, but there was Mom, standing beside him, agreeing! Didn't she remember how hard we had worked to pack the trailer the first time, I was wondering! Of course, I couldn't say anything out loud for fear of getting my attitude changed by my uncle reaching out and me trying to duck! I then had the kids come in to help too because if I was going to suffer through this, they were going to learn hard work too! After what seemed like the whole day, we finally had it to their (my mom's and uncle's) liking. I was ready for bed!

Picture of trailer after my brother repacked it.

Keith just had the knowledge and the ability to pack the trailer better than we ever could have by ourselves. The next morning, we were up and on the go again, bidding my brother and sister-in-law farewell, not knowing if I would ever see him or them again.

My brother, Keith and sister-in-law, Jo

I was going to miss his absolutely wonderful home and the scenery from his back porch. It was breathtaking because they had built on the shoals, and the house overlooks a little river and cow pasture. I fell in love with the area and could see why they had chosen that place to build. We spent two nights in Texas, having driven a total of three days to arrive near the border. We arrived in Brownsville, Texas, early in the afternoon, which gave us some relaxing time before we had to cross the border the next morning. We were up the next morning, had breakfast, and packed some food with us for traveling with two kids. We were both very nervous and very scared at the prospect of crossing the border.

Crossing the Border

We drove through the town of Brownsville, Texas, on our way to the border and crossed into Matamoros, Mexico. Laurel was driving her car with Trenton riding with her, and I was driving my truck with Brittnay and Fargo with me. We pulled up to the first tower after crossing into Mexico. We were all so very nervous, scared, panicky, excited, mostly scared though; I think it was because we had no idea what to expect. There was a person sitting in the tower, and he waved us over to the next tower. I was hauling the eight-foot trailer, and if you have ever backed up an eight-foot trailer, they do not back up very easily. They never go in a straight line regardless of whether you touch your steering wheel or not. I had been backing up my horse trailer for several years and could usually put it most any place that I wanted it to go. Not this trailer; it had a mind of its own! I started backing it up, and it started going every which way but straight! I finally made my way over to the next tower, and they motioned for me to go to the next one! I began to wonder if they were playing a game with me! I had to back up again, and by this time, I had semi trucks that were starting to line up behind me. The truck drivers were not too happy with me to say the least! I finally got to the correct entrance. Yeah! I was very nervous and did not have a clue what to expect or what was expected of me. Not much at that point, and we then eventually had to drive over to this building with parking and a little shade. That was a good thing because by then, it was in the nineties, and I had a frantically panting rottweiler behind me drooling and moving around and wanting to know what the heck was going on. I rolled down the windows about one-third of the way on each side. I slid open the back sliding window and popped open the back windows. They only opened about two inches, but at that point, anything would help hopefully. Laurel and I both took our papers that we thought that we might need, our vehicle titles, our list of items, our passports, Laurel's FM3, the dog's medical records including his rabies certificate and health certificate from Lansing. We were ready! We walked in, and of course, no one spoke English. We made it through getting our passports checked and the dog's papers checked and were okayed. We then had to go to another window across the way and stand in line for our vehicles. At this point, we met some other Americans, two guys and a woman. The woman was Mexican, and she was the wife of one of the guys. They had a load of stuff in their truck and were trying to write a list as they were standing there while she was translating it for them. At least we already had that done! We got to the window for the vehicles and got sent over to another building to have copies made—everything had to be done in triplicate. We got that done and went back. We stood in line again and finally got through and paid our import taxes on our vehicles and received our *plactas* for our vehicles. This is a very important piece of paper, and you must put the sticker in the left bottom of your windshield and keep the paper that was issued with it. Of course, we were not told this, or maybe we were and did not understand. It was all so very traumatic that it is hard to remember everything you are being told or shown. We then were able to go out by our vehicles. After we got our passports stamped, as well as our tourist visas, the dog's papers, and the vehicle permits, we thought that we were done. We all got in our cars and headed out of the parking area. At the end of the parking area was a big green and red light post. Before we made it to that point, a guard stopped us and told us we could not proceed. Of course, we didn't understand what was going on because he only spoke Spanish. We were blocking the exit, and we finally figured out that there was something more needed. I then had to back up again and go back to my original parking spot. This was not an easy task with a *big* panting dog blocking my view, what little view I had, and the trailer that does not like to back up in a straight line. After I finished parking again, I then let Fargo out and asked where I could take him to go to the bathroom. I gave him a drink of water, and then we all sat in the parking lot in the shade and ate our peanut butter sandwiches that we had packed for lunch. Fargo lay out there with us as we ate, but he sure was miserable and hot!

Eventually, we were approached by this nice young man who spoke English. We had no idea who or what he was, but he told us that we were going to have to pay a tax on our belongings that we brought across with us. The closest thing that I can think of to describe the young man is that he was like a broker. He always referred to his bosses, and he would have to take things to his boss for approval such as our translated list of our belongings that we had already paid to have approved in Detroit. He asked us what we thought our things were worth. When he asked us this question, we had no idea that we had to pay an import tax on our belongings. We were honest with him and told him what we thought they were worth. He then said, "Well, don't you think that they could be worth a little less, such as this amount?" and he quoted a certain amount.

We said, "Okay, yes," and he then had to go talk to his boss. About one and a half hours later, he returned. This went on for quite a while; we then had to pay a certain amount in cash. Unfortunately, I did not write that amount down and do not remember how much we paid. Around 2:00 or 3:00 p.m., he came out and told me that I would have to take my truck and trailer over to another area where they would check my belongings in my truck and trailer. I could not understand where he was trying to tell me to go, so I unloaded Fargo and left him with Laurel and the kids, and the guy came with me. We had to cross over all the lanes and ended up where all the semi trucks, I am assuming, got checked. It was like a long, very high loading dock. The guy told me that I would have to pay the inspector to come out and take a look and approve my load. I would also be expected to tip the guys that unpack everything. I was over there all by myself; luckily, I still had the two-way radio with me. I had to wait for quite some time before anyone came out. Then all these guys came out, and I was the only woman around anywhere. Great! I was very glad that I was six feet tall and muscular from all the horse and barn work I had been doing most of my life. I was very uncomfortable being there by myself, and then the guys jumped down and started untying, unsnapping, and unbuckling everything. They took both bikes off and took the tarp off. Thank God they left it screwed to the front; they just threw it over the front. The first thing that they found was my chain saw. Then they all started talking to each other at once. I can only imagine what they were thinking and saying! Don't ask why I took my chain saw; it was only because Kevin had told me that he had a jungle by his house that we could trim up with it. They took several boxes down and opened them up, but not as many as I expected. They then got into the back of my truck. They only removed about three boxes and opened them. It was around 4:00 p.m. by this time and hotter than a pistol, and they were tired and hot from working all day. That is probably why they only took out and opened a few of the boxes. After checking these boxes, they then closed them up, put them back in my truck, and proceeded to repack my trailer and cover it up again. Well, it certainly was not like my brother had done it, but at this point, what is a girl to do? I did try to direct them as to how to put back the bikes and retie them on. I then tipped them $10 each, and we were ready to go after I paid my fee to the inspector. The broker and I got into my truck, and he started telling me what we would have to do. He told me to drive up to the first tower slowly but not too slow and not too fast. *What does that mean exactly?* I was thinking but did not say anything and had to figure it out for myself. Once you get to the tower, you either get a green light, which means you can go through, or you get a red light, which means you stop and they go through everything again. We made it through the first light. He was then talking to me and explaining what we needed to do next. Laurel broke in on the two-way, yelling about her predicament over on the other side. It seems that they did not want to let her through because she did not have any of the paperwork with her, and she had to cram the dog and both kids in her car with everything else that she had packed in there. We did not have a clue that I would not be returning for Fargo to put him back into my truck! I was trying to talk to her and make sense of what she was telling me, and the broker told me to be quiet and listen to him! We were approaching the second light tower. Laurel started screaming at me for help; he was yelling at me to drive slowly, and thank God we made it through the second light! By then, they had let Laurel, the kids, and the dog through, and she was driving on the highway not knowing where she was or where I was. I finally got through the *third* light, yes three of them, and we were on our way on the highway also not knowing where Laurel was either. I finally got a glimpse of her car, and she actually ended up behind me. We ended up out on a six-lane highway with hardly a place to pull over. I finally was able to stop to let the broker out of my truck. I paid him US $50 for his help, got Fargo, and we were on our way. Where, we did not have a clue! We ended up turning around and started heading the other way. We were looking for a place to pull over to retie everything down because by then, things were looking pretty bad because the tarp was flapping and things were ready to fall out into the street. We finally spotted a fenced parking lot that I thought that I could maneuver around. We pulled in and got out and started to retie things, and this guy came out and told us that we had to leave because they were closing and the gate would be shut and locked. We asked him if he knew where this certain hotel that we had booked reservations was, and he did not know. Just then, a woman came out, and he asked her if she knew. She did know, and she spoke a little English so was able to give us specific directions. We had to leave that parking lot, however, without being able to secure everything before we pulled out. We proceeded down the highway until we finally were able to pull over, and we did the best we could until we reached our destination for the night. We then had to turn around again because we needed to go in the opposite direction toward the hotel.

We were heading into the town of Matamoros, which was quite a harrowing experience in itself having never driven in Mexico before! One thing that was very different for us is that their stoplights are on the side of the streets where ours hang overhead in the middle of the intersection. It took me quite a few intersections before I began to adjust to the new way, having driven through many red lights while adjusting with Laurel watching behind me in her car having little panic attacks every time I drove through one! Luckily, I did not get hit that first day while trying to adjust. All of the streets were one way, so if we missed something, we had to drive around and around to figure out how to get back to where we wanted to be. The streets were so narrow that my truck and trailer hardly fit through some of them. We ended up driving past the parking lot for the hotel, but we did not realize it was parking for the hotel because it really was not near the hotel. We then passed the hotel, and Laurel told me that she thought that the parking lot that we had passed was probably for the hotel guests. We had to go all the way around again because of the one-way streets. We eventually made it into the parking lot, and I then had to back my trailer up back into a certain spot quite precisely where the parking attendant wanted me to park. We were all out around my truck and trailer once I got it parked, and this taxi drove by with this guy hanging out the window. Trenton yelled, "I think that that was Enrique," and sure enough, it was. How about that for good timing? Coincidence? Laurel and Enrique walked over to the hotel to check in, and they found out that the hotel did not allow dogs. Enrique suggested that we just leave Fargo tied outside the truck or inside the truck for the night by himself. He knew absolutely nothing about how American dogs were raised and treated! He could not believe it when I told him there was no way that Fargo was going to stay in the truck by himself not even mentioning tying him up outside and just leaving him! He did not understand what the problem was because the less fortunate culture basically lets the dog fend for itself, and if you have a dog, it is for your protection of your belongings. The dog's job is to take care of you, not the other way around. I quickly informed Enrique that Fargo was my baby and that I would never leave him anywhere alone! I told him that I would sleep out in the truck with Fargo, and that is when he volunteered to stay out with Fargo and watch over our belongings as well. Trenton wanted to stay out there with him, and Laurel let him do so. Needless to say, they did not get much sleep, including Fargo, nor did I knowing that Fargo was out there and I was inside.

Adventure through Mexico

O n our first morning in Mexico, before we started out anywhere, I insisted that we find an insurance office because I wanted to put insurance on my truck. I had heard so many horror stories about driving in Mexico. I was scared and did not want to be without insurance. As soon as you cross the border with your vehicle, your insurance is no longer valid. We found an office, and we all went in with Enrique translating for us. I ended up paying $165 for two weeks worth of insurance! I could have bought insurance at the border as we were doing our paperwork; however, I didn't because I thought it was too expensive. As it turned out, it didn't matter whether I had bought it at the border or in the town of Matamoros; I paid the same expensive price! Lesson learned.

After buying my insurance, we were on our way. We had a map that comes in the back of the book of maps that you can buy of the United States, Canada and Mexico. thinking that would be good enough to get us through Mexico; however, we did not have a map of the city, so we just headed south. We eventually found the highway that we needed, and away we went. One thing that I regret is that I did not keep track of the cities where we spent the nights; however, I did record the money spent on gas, tolls, and hotels. The first day of our trip was very brown and barren. I remember just seeing brown because the trees were brown, the dirt was brown, the houses were basically brown, the stick houses with palapa roofs were brown, and the people were brown. That is what my impression of my first sights are of being in Mexico.

It was very hot, and Fargo was very uncomfortable unless we were moving with the air on. When we would stop at a gas station and let him out, there were never any shade trees to take him under for relief from the blistering sun. I was afraid to explore with him a little as I did not want to offend anyone or go somewhere that I was not supposed to be; therefore, I basically stayed near the gas station for him to do his duty. The first day when we stopped for lunch, it was along the highway because we had planned on stopping for a nice picnic lunch. There was a place to pull over, but when we got out, we discovered that the whole place was filled with everyone else's garbage. I could not let Fargo wander a bit because I had to be careful about where he was stepping and what he was sniffing. We made our peanut butter and jam sandwiches once again and ate quickly to get out of there. So much for our nice picnic lunch! On the second night in Mexico, we finally found a place that would let us take Fargo inside with us. They were little cabins with two beds and a bathroom with a window air conditioner. We were told that dogs were not supposed to be there, so we were supposed to try to keep Fargo out of site. *How do you hide a 130-pound Rottweiler?* I was thinking. Poor Fargo, he had been raised in the country where he could run in the fields and go to the bathroom wherever he wanted. I also had had a fenced yard, so being on a leash all the time or having his bathroom roaming space constricted because he was supposed to be out of site was very hard on him.

My truck and trailer had to be parked about one hundred fifty feet from the cabin, which was much further away than I felt comfortable with, but that was the only place that I could park it. During the night, with the air conditioner running, Fargo started growling his very deep growl and barking his mean bark. I got up and turned the porch light on, opened the door, and looked outside toward my truck. I did not see anything or anybody around my truck, so I very naively turned the light out and went back to bed. The next morning when we went to leave, we saw that someone during the night had tried to help themselves to our belongings. They had some of the ropes cut and some of the bungee cords undone but not any of the heavy-duty ratchet straps. They hadn't counted on Fargo hearing them and warning me, but apparently hearing his bark was enough to scare them away. There was a large grocery store across the street from the motel, so Laurel and I walked over to it and bought some snacks and drinks and food. This town happened to have a McDonalds in it, so we went to McDonalds for breakfast.

Day two involved driving, driving, and more driving. When we stopped for lunch, we were in a town with a river running through it. We went to an open-air restaurant on the river and asked if we could bring the dog with us. They said that we could, so I went back to the truck and got my poor baby out of the truck, and he got to relax with us at the restaurant. It was a very nice place, and the food was delicious. It was so nice just being able to get out of the truck and car and be able to take Fargo someplace in the shade so that he could stretch out when he lay down. I forgot to mention that once we picked up Enrique, I had to take both kids in my truck. Brittnay sat in the passenger seat, and poor Trenton got put in the back with Fargo. I had the backseat flipped up so that Fargo could have more room, and he and Trenton were constantly in a struggle for space. It became a war between them as to who was going to be able to be where. We had had to pack so full that Laurel's backseat was full up to the back window to the point of not being able to see out of her back window. I not only had the kids, the dog, and myself but we also had stuff in the truck as well. Every time that I needed to get out, it was a struggle. I also had maps and papers on the dashboard. We were packed so full, I don't think I could have added a bottle of water! Therefore, when we could all get out and stretch and relax in the shade for a while, it was very much appreciated. After lunch, we all crammed back into the vehicles and bid the town farewell. We had been driving twelve to fourteen hours per day. On the third night out, we started looking fairly early in the day for a hotel that would allow Fargo to be with us. We had stopped in this one town for dinner where we couldn't find a place to park in the shade for Fargo. I ended up parking and putting sunshades in the front windshield and on both side windows leaving them down about five inches. The temperature was around ninety-five degrees at this time of day, but I was afraid to leave the windows down any further for fear that someone might try to bother or steal Fargo. We found a restaurant within the sight of the truck; unfortunately, my steak that I had ordered after having waited for quite some time for our food was spoiled. I went without dinner that night. By 10:00 p.m. that evening, we still had not found a hotel that would allow me to bring Fargo in with us. We were entering this town, and there was a bridge to cross. Laurel had gotten quite a bit further down the road than I, and I lost track of where she had gone. I called her on the radio to see where she was, but by then, she was out of range. We were separated for about twenty minutes or so; that seemed like hours in hell for me because I was scared and got quite frantic! I finally just pulled off the road and sat and let them find me because of the trailer.

We finally connected once again and decided to try and find a hotel in that town as it was around 11:00 p.m., and we were all very tired and stressed from the trip itself and from being separated. The hotel where we stopped would not let Fargo in with us, so I decided, rather than to continue looking for a different hotel, that I would stay out in the truck with him. The mosquitoes were absolutely horrendous. I sat outside with him and let him lie in the grass for quite a while where it was cooler for him and me. I finally could not take the mosquitoes any longer and was concerned at being outside by ourselves, so we got back into the truck. Fargo did not want to be in the back; he wanted to be in the front with me. It was very hot and humid, and all he could do was pant and drool, which kind of goes together in a Rottweiler. We did not get much sleep to say the least. In the morning, Laurel came out after her shower and stayed with Fargo so that I could go in and take a shower and change clothes. I was covered in mosquito bites from head to toes. My toes were even covered with red spots! I looked like I had the measles. We left the hotel and were on the road again, being near the state of Veracruz at the time. Veracruz is very lush and green and very hilly or mountainous. We were in mountains for almost two days, and by the end of those hills, I was running out of brakes. I had had electric brakes for my horse trailer, but I did not think that I would need them for the little eight-foot trailer. I hadn't given any thought to the amount of weight that was going to be in my truck and trailer, so I did not have electric brakes installed on the trailer. As we were driving through these hills, Laurel and Enrique were cruising in front of us quite carefree it seemed while I was looking for a place to pull over and take a break since we all needed one at this point—we that were jammed into the truck, that is! I hadn't said anything to Laurel via the walkie-talkie, so when I spotted this kind of dirt road pull-off place, I did so without Laurel's knowledge. By that time, she was out of radio range again, but I had to stop! We had to get out of that truck! I figured that eventually she and Enrique would discover that I was no longer behind them and turn around. The little dirt road that I thought was a road was actually someone's driveway, and there were kids playing down the hill and into the jungle area. We stayed there for a little while; then Laurel and Enrique came back for us, and we were all able to relax a bit before packing ourselves back into the truck.

Picture of the horse wandering loose in the street
that is described in my book. Trip Down

During our trip, we were driving through this little town and
saw a horse just wandering the streets like a dog. It didn't even
have a halter on or anything; it was just in town hanging out, too
funny. We also saw many horses along the way tied out along
the road with just a rope tied around their necks. They were out
there, eating grass along the highway, but they were tied so close
to the road that is was scary for me being a horse owner. Things
like these have become very common to me, so I have to try to
remember to include these little tidbits because it is not normal
for us Americans to see. We saw many burros, and we also saw
cowboys on their horses herding cattle down the roads. This is an
abnormal sight for me being from Michigan. On one particular
time, we went by three guys and their horses. The cowboys were
tying their horses in the jungle bushes and heading across the
road to the Corona building. There are little Corona or Superior
stores all along the roads throughout Mexico. If you cannot find
anything else, you can always find a cerveza. Another time we
saw a cowboy riding his horse and leading another all saddled
and bridled like he was just waiting for someone to come along

and go for a ride with him. You have no idea how badly I wanted to stop and ask if I could take a ride! I told Laurel, "There is my cowboy waiting for me with a horse for me to ride and everything." Unfortunately, it was not in my destiny or at our destination. One time there was a family that stopped along the road with a horse, and they were all standing under a shade tree. We stopped so that I could get out and go see the horse. I gave it an apple, but he would not eat it. It probably had never seen an apple before, and the people were looking at me like I was some kind of person that just plopped down from outer space. They probably had never seen anyone like me before either as I am six feet tall and blonde. They just looked at me, and after the horse wouldn't eat the apple, I felt kind of foolish. It wasn't the first time that I had that feeling and was sure that it would not be my last!

Picture of me (Ruth) when I stopped to give the
apple to the horse on the side of the road.

We were just getting out of the mountainous area and were seeing seashore. We did not know it at the time, but we were just north of the city of Veracruz. We spotted this two-story resort-type motel by the ocean. It had a swimming pool, and it also had a spacious area to park the truck and trailer. It was early, around 4:00 p.m. or so. We all needed a little downtime and some relief from being so crowded and cramped up. We stopped and asked if they took dogs. Lo and behold, they did. We checked in, and the kids went immediately to the pool. Laurel, Enrique, and I also went, and I was able to take Fargo with me. First, I took him out to the beach for a walk. The sand was really weird, kind of black-looking and mushy when you walked on it. I let him run for a bit until he was tired. He did not venture into the water and neither did I. We went to the pool area so I could go swimming and relax my poor body for a while. Boy, it sure felt good! We swam and played around in the water for quite a while. It was such a nice place, and it had such a nice breeze blowing. The palm trees were swaying in the breeze, and no one else was there, so we kind of had the place to ourselves. The next morning, all too soon, we were back in the truck and car and on the road again. The highway leveled out, so that was a good thing. I still had brakes; that was the main thing!

We traveled all day and ended up staying the night in Campeche. This town is quite large and is on the water also. It is a fishing town, and I do not know what else. It had quite a few large buildings in the town, and we did manage, once again, to find a hotel that would let Fargo in. There was a walled area for the truck and trailer and car. They had a night guard, so that was good. We got put on the main floor, so it was much easier to take Fargo in and out to go to the bathroom. The next morning as we were getting ready to leave, Laurel had locked her keys in the car! Oh great! No hideaway key, of course, no spare key anywhere! Luckily, Enrique was able to break in with a coat hanger. Laurel and I took Fargo and went for a walk along the river to look over the town a little. I found a bank and needed to get change for a one-hundred-dollar bill. It was not as simple as you would think. I had to go back to the hotel and get my passport. We all loaded up in the vehicles and drove over to the bank. I went in with my passport, waited in line for quite some time, and finally got my change. What an ordeal for just $100!

Enrique had warned us that driving between Campeche and Merida was and could be very dangerous. He warned us not to stop for anyone, only the army at a border check. He was very adamant about this, and he acted scared himself! Enrique's brother was a special forces cop in Cancun. If you have been down there, they were guys that dress all in black. Those were the guys. His brother is the one who warned him, so he took it seriously. He drove in front, and I was to follow very close. We hit rain that day, and we were driving with a purpose that day if you get my drift. We made it through with no problems. This is a good place to tell about border checks. There are a lot of them when you drive through Mexico. The guys are usually dressed in army uniforms, carrying machine guns and *not* friendly. Laurel and Enrique got checked four times. They had to pull over and unpack the whole car! I, on the other hand, never got checked even though I had the truck filled to the hilt and pulling the trailer. They would take one look at Fargo in the backseat and tell me to go ahead. Fargo was good for a lot of things! With everything that could have happened to us on the way down with our vehicles or our persons, we were very blessed.

The good Lord took very good care of us, and we arrived in Cancun at 5:30 p.m. on the fifth day of traveling in Mexico. Enrique led us straight to our rental house, and we were home at last. There were a bunch of kids playing soccer in the park near the house. As soon as Trenton could get out of the truck and get his soccer ball, he was over there, playing with the kids. We spent the evening unpacking the truck and trailer, setting up beds, fixing something to eat, and collapsing. We shoved the trailer into the gated area in the front of the house. Laurel also parked her car in there. I parked my truck in the street right in front of the house. We locked the bikes to one of the palm trees in the front yard. Trenton had been warned over and over again to always bring in his Rollerblades, skateboard, or whatever he had been playing with at the time inside the house when he was finished with them.

When we finally arrived in Cancun, our boat still was not there. Carlos, whom we had contracted with to bring the boat down, had been trying to get it there. He had already, by this time, flown to Miami twice to try to bring the boat over. Both times after he arrived in Miami, a storm came in, and he was unable to sail it over. So now we are in Cancun, our business is in Cancun, but our boat is not. Very shortly after our arrival, Fargo got deathly ill. His kidneys were failing, and I came very close to loosing him. Kevin had a very good vet down there, and I called him. They actually make house calls if your animal is too sick to come into the office. Hector is the veterinarian, and he was another angel that God sent to us as far as I am concerned. He put Fargo on medicine and also gave him some kind of holistic pill and had us get cranberry juice to mix with water. He could not keep dog food down at this point; it was in the ninety to one hundred degrees in temperature and very humid. Luckily, our house had a lot of shade around it. I bought a floor fan for Fargo only, and he had this fan until the day we packed and left. Not too many days after Fargo got sick, I got sick also. I do not know if it was from all the mosquito bites or what it was, but I was really, really sick. At one point, I was lying on the floor in front of the fan with Fargo and slept. It was so hot and miserable. Laurel ended up taking care of both of us. She was a very good caretaker of both of us. Fargo would not have made it if it were not for her care and the kids taking care of him also. His urine was very dark, and at one point, the vet told me that if his urine turned black, he was all done. Thank God, it never did get black. Slowly but surely, he started getting better. I on the other hand, I seemed to be getting worse. I was still sick in July when the boat arrived. Laurel and Carlos took care of everything. I would be okay sometimes and then get deathly ill again. I was not even able to go out to see the boat when she arrived into Cancun. The boat was taken to the Hacienda del Mar and docked there until it was checked into customs. As I recall, the boat was at the Hacienda del Mar for about three to four weeks. Laurel had to go with Carlos out to the airport and take care of the paperwork out there. I think we applied for the first permit before the boat actually arrived and then had to wait.

While we were waiting for the boat to arrive, I started applying for my FM3, my visa to live in Mexico and run our business. Laurel had already been through this, so she started doing my papers, copying from hers. That way, Kevin did not have to come in with us every time that we needed to go into immigration. It was a very interesting place to sit and observe people and the immigration office. I am a people watcher, so I would occupy myself, observing other people while we were waiting our turn. The system of getting into the office is, you go early in the morning and hope that you can get a parking place anywhere near the office. You then stand outside and try to keep track of the people that were there before you and after you. As it is nearing the time for the office to open, a line starts to form near the door. The closer to the opening time, the more frantic the line is. If you are there for the first time, you try to be fair and not get in front of anyone that was there before you. That lasts for only the first time that you are there. The second and any time thereafter, you live by their motto of "survival of the fittest." When it is time to get in line, you rush to get in line ahead of as many people as you can! As you then enter the office, you are issued a number. You are then taken by the number that you have sort of like at the meat counter in a grocery store. They only take so many numbers for the day, and then you are out of luck. You come back the next day, and it starts all over again. They only take people from 8:00 a.m. until 2:00 p.m. One plus to the waiting is it is air-conditioned in there, and there is a bathroom. Actually, that is two plusses. When you first apply, your American passport is taken from you and kept until you are issued your FM3. That at first is kind of troublesome, giving up your passport. When you are applying for your FM3 and own a business, they have to have a copy of your acta. The acta is a very important document, and everyone needs a copy of your acta before they can do anything for you. If you want to open a bank account, they need your acta because we were business owners; everything was more complicated. They ended up, after about three weeks, having a problem with our acta. Kevin ended up going in with me two or three times, and we were actually thinking that they were not going to issue me my FM3. After several arguments on Kevin's part, I finally received it.

Finding a Captain

It now became time to find a captain. Kevin helped us put an AD in the two main papers down there. They had Kevin's phone number to call, and he would set up the appointments to interview them. Once again, the responsibility fell on Laurel's and Kevin's shoulders. I was ill again. They did a few interviews, and we picked out the very overqualified (we thought) captain from Germany to come out and sail the boat. The boat, at this time, was still at the Hacienda del Mar. The dock at the Hacienda is shaped like a big T; only at the end of one of the T's the dock winds around and curves. So inside, it is almost like a circle. Boats are docked on both sides of the long part of the T and at both ends of the T inside and out. Inside of the circle, kind of at the end, was our boat. On the other end of the same half of the T, there were two *big* wooden pirate ships named the *Nina* and *Pinta*. The time was set; this was going to be our first ride out on our new boat. We had the kids, Laurel, Kevin, and a friend that I had met whose name was Torito, which is "little bull" in Spanish. His nickname was not Torito for nothing. He was a bodybuilder and about six feet tall. Thank God we had him out on the boat that very first day. He had never been out on a boat before, so it was his first time out on any boat. Well, the captain put up the main, the genoa, started the motor, and untied the boat. Oh my God, we started full speed not out toward the open seas. No, we were heading straight toward one of the big wooden ships. When I realized he did not have control, I was yelling at him, and he was yelling orders to us in his German/Spanish accent. I jumped up and popped the genoa sheet and yanked it down. Laurel got to the motor and got that turned off. Torito jumped out on the edge of one of the pontoons and stuck out his very powerful arms and stopped our boat from ramming into the ship. It was only by the grace of God that Torito was on that boat and that he did not fall off the hull. We all recovered from the almost tragedy; the captain was a nervous wreck and so were we! He did get the boat turned around, and this time, he did not put up the sails until we were out into the sea. You think? He did take us out for a nice sail, and we did get the boat back safely. However, we did not call him back. Laurel and Kevin interviewed a few more guys, and she ruled it down to a couple for a second interview so that I could meet them. By then, I was feeling a little better again. There was this one named Ceasar that she said showed up and spilled his drink all over the table, and he was so nervous. She was not that impressed with him, but we met with him again. I talked with him and didn't think he was so bad. We also interviewed another guy that same evening. We asked Ceasar to come out and sail the boat for us. When his day came to come out, our motor was not working. He did not seem to think that that was going to be a problem and sailed it away from the dock. He took us out sailing and managed to sail the boat back to the dock and dock it all under sail. Well, we were quite impressed. The problem with finding a captain down there is that not very many of them know how to sail. They all know how to motor a boat, but that is not what we wanted to offer our people. We had been out on enough of the sailboats down there that would put up a sail but never shut off their motor. So you would go out sailing but not really sailing. The only captain that we had been with that actually sailed was Palemon. Another problem with the captains down there is hardly any of them are fluent in English. Our AD asked for 75 percent English-speaking skill, but most of the guys that Laurel interviewed did not even speak 40–50 percent English. We needed an English-speaking captain for two reasons. We wanted him to be able to communicate with our clients and we also needed to communicate. So after Cesar's sailing demonstration and since he was also 100 percent English-speaking skill, we decided on him.

We hired him and put him to work working on the maintenance of the boat. You see, once the boat was checked into the Mexican government as a tourist boat, the boat needed a captain to move the boat. The boat could not be moved by us even if we knew how to do it. That is why we hired a captain so early in the whole process. If a hurricane should come up, someone was needed to take care of the boat.

Lalo, Laurel and Trenton shortly after we got the boat to Cancun.

About this same time, we decided that we needed a marketing person. Laurel and I were just not going to cut it. Laurel had planned on doing the marketing, and I planned on doing the accounting part of it while both of us would run the whole thing together. We had dreams of eliminating the travel agencies and going straight to the personal concierges at the hotels. Most of the travel agencies down in Cancun get 40–60 percent of ticket sales. Us being a new company, with not much to fall back on, wanted to try to make as much as possible to try and get out of debt. This, we thought, would be a good way to get to the people and let them know that we were there. We thought once people found out about us being Americans and all, they would come flocking to our boat. So we hired Charlie and made him our marketing man. He soon became our Mexican partner as well. Enrique just did not work out for us, and it was not a good idea to keep him as a partner. Charlie had a college education and came from a very good family. He was from the upper class and entirely a different kind of person than we had been dealing with so far. We had no doubts that he would be okay for us to make as a partner, and if we were wrong, we were covered anyway.

About this time, as soon as our boat had been checked through with the harbor master and immigration, we were able to move the boat to the restaurant. First, we needed to go and talk to the owner with whom we had a contract. Kevin, Laurel, and I went out to Punta Sam to talk to him and let him know that we were ready to move the boat. We walked into the restaurant, and of course, he did not even remember who we were. As I stated before, I am six feet tall and blonde. Laurel is a blonde also but not as tall, which she is very thankful for I might add. The señor did not remember us once again! *Give me a break*, I thought to myself. Kevin let him know that our boat was in Cancun and that we were ready to move it. When we had made the contract with him, he told us that he would install running water out on the dock and also power and lights. Were they done? Nope! Nada, zip, not. We talked with him about it, and again, he stated that he would have it done. We moved the boat out to Punta Sam and hoped for the best. Since we were not going to run our tours to Isla Contoy and we did not have a snorkeling permit from Semernap yet and did not know when one would be issued, we needed to find a place to take our tourists snorkeling. Our new captain told us about a reef called Meca Loco out of Puerto Juarez. We took a trip out there, and when he found it, we all went snorkeling to check it out. Actually, it was a very nice reef with a lot of sea life and pretty and various coral. It was a perfect place for us since our boat was out in this area anyway. Things were coming together slowly but surely.

During this time, we also started applying for our permits that we needed. Kevin went into the harbor master's office with us and once again got a list of all the permits that we would need. He helped us fill out the paperwork for the first permit needed. We went back the next day to turn it in. The harbor master, like immigration, do not look at what you have turned into them at the time that you turn it in. You have to return when you are told. This was the beginning of one of our nightmares! At first, for about the first year or so, we were not accepted at all. When you go up to the window after waiting your turn, you most always get a different person compared to the one you had the last time in. They all kind of sat back, you might say, observed us, and waited to see what kind of people we were. We turned in our first application, were given a day to return, returned, was rejected for some reason or another, and this goes on and on and on. We finally were able to get the first permit. Then we had to apply for the second. That one did not come any easier than the first. By now, we are getting kind of frantic because we cannot work until we have all seven permits. We originally had plans of getting the boat there, get the permits, work awhile, and maybe pull the boat out in November and have it repainted. Huh! What dreamers we were and very foolish. All the while that we are waiting and trying to get the permits, we did other things also. Charlie needed pictures of the boat, so one day, we went out for the day, and Kevin took pictures of the boat from our little dingy that we had to have before trying to cross from Florida to Cancun. We were out most of the day, taking all kinds of pictures with the sails up in the beautiful blue waters and into the evening to get pictures of the boat in the sunset.

That was way too much fun. On one week, we decided to take a little trip to Chetumal and Belize. We also wanted to go to Mahaul. Kevin told me that he would take care of my dogs as long as Fargo would let him in the house. We had to make sure before we left that he would indeed allow that, and he did. We packed up and took Laurel's car because it was much cheaper on gas, and by then, my insurance had run out on my truck, I could not afford other insurance and was afraid to drive my truck without insurance. That meant that we were driving Laurel's car a lot! On the way to Chetumal, we decided to give Brittnay some driving time since she was fifteen and needed to learn how to drive. I was in the front seat with her since my legs are so long and my feet are so long that it was hard for me to fit anywhere else. That is one advantage that I have anyway; I usually always get to sit in the front. Britt was driving and never had driven along a highway before at such speed. I was forced to grab the steering wheel a couple of times to keep us from running off the road, but she soon got the hang of it. She now drives like Laurel and I do with kind of a lead foot and with confidence. If you do not have confidence in your ability or yourself, forget driving down there. They will drive you off the road and keep you there!

We arrived at Chetumal and checked in with immigration since we were leaving Mexico. We got our passports stamped and everything that we needed for the car and drove across the border once again. We then had to check in once we got over the bridge and to immigration at Belize. We all went in to have our passports stamped and get what we needed for the car. We did not have a really good warm, fuzzy feeling going into the immigration office if you know what I mean and were not treated exactly too warm either. We were informed that we would have to put insurance on the car and pay import tax and also would have to exchange our pesos for their currency. There were several booths and guys outside the building hanging around wanting to exchange our money. We decided that this was not exactly what we wanted to do, so we got into the car and drove back across the border into Mexico. There are places that you can park your vehicle and walk across the border into the free zone of shopping in Belize, and that is what we did. We had to find out what we had to do since we checked out of Mexico and all, but it turned out not to be a big deal. We spent a few hours shopping, bought some bottles of alcohol since it is very cheap over there, and returned to our car. We spent the night in Chetumal, which is the capital of the state of Quintana-Roo, Mexico. The next day, we headed out for Mahaul. It is off the main drag quite a ways but was very worth the extra miles. It was (I do not know what it looks like now.) a very little village, and the main road ran along the beach in the sand.

Trenton running down the "main road" in Mahual.

There was one hotel there, and there were a couple of little stores, dive shop, a little village, and a really cool place to visit. We got a room and spent the night. The hotel also had a little restaurant, so there was a place to eat. We just loved it there but, unfortunately, were never able to return. Someday, I would like to go back.

On the south end of the village apart from the village, there was a huge modern shopping mall and a ship dock where cruise ships came into the port and the people were dropped off to shop. This huge mall was for cruise ship people only. At that time we were there, it was just beginning to be developed for housing; we guessed it was for the workers. I sure would have liked to have had enough money to buy land and start a horseback riding facility. We drove back the next day, stopping at a few more cool places on the way. It was a very interesting trip, and it was my only trip for the whole four years that I lived down there except for the trip down and the trip back. We just never had the time nor the money to do much while we were there except try to make a go of it.

Two weeks after we hired Cesar, our captain, he convinced us that we needed to hire a first mate. We were very naive and vulnerable and open to all requests from our captain. We put another AD in the papers, this time, for a first mate. We were asking, once again, for sailing experience and 70 percent English-speaking skill. Laurel, once again, was responsible for the interviews as I was still sick or sick again. It kind of all blends together after awhile. Cesar told us of a friend of his by the name of Pablo, who at that time was working for Aqua World, the biggest boat company down there. Laurel and Kevin interviewed him the first time, and I was there for the second interview. He was very uncertain of quitting his job and coming to work for us. This all probably was an act at that time to get more money from us, but who knows. We offered him double what he had been making at Aqua World, better working conditions, and less hours. He finally agreed to come and work for us. This meant that we now had three full-time employees and no work.

We needed to go over to Isla Mujeres and talk with the owner of the restaurant that we had eaten at every time that we had gone over there as tourists. We had our captain and our new first mate sail us over there one fine day to check things out. The captain told us of another restaurant that some of the boats used, and we decided to check that one out first. We sailed there first and talked with the owner about the food and the prices. We also checked out the facilities and then went sailing on our way over to the next dock that was closer to where we needed to go. We got very close to the dock, our motor quite running, and guess what boat we almost hit? Yup, the pirate ship was docked near, and we almost hit it again! As it was, we got our main stay caught on a piece of their boat that stuck out, but we were able to become untangled without any damage to either boat. We really needed to avoid these boats like the plague! We got safely docked, and Laurel and I walked to the restaurant to talk to the owner. He was very nice to us and gave us a very fair price per person. Their food was always excellent every time that we had eaten there, and that is where we wanted to bring our people. We told him we did not know exactly when we would be starting, but he told us to just let him know when we were ready to start. Alfredo has since then become one of our very dear friends down there. Since the boat was docked out in Punta Sam, we needed to find a van service to hire to bring our clients out to the boat and back again. It was just way out of the way to expect any tourist to be able to find their way out there. Charlie, our marketing person, had a friend that was just starting up a van service down there. Charlie called him for us and set up a time for him to bring one of the vans by for us to look at. We inspected the van; it was brand-new, and we set up a contract with him per van. If we were lucky and filled the boat, we would at some point need all three of his vans.

It got to the point that we were very uncomfortable at the restaurant out in Punta Sam. The owner still had not put running water out to the dock nor had he installed any lighting. We started looking for a different place to dock. I had Kevin go with us one day, and we stopped at a little restaurant that we had been driving past when we went out to Punta Sam. The restaurant was in Puerto Juarez and was just a little place, but it had a reasonably nice dock, and the restaurant had a bathroom. The dock also had running water out to it, which was a big plus. We spoke to the owner, looked over the dock to make sure that there was enough draw for our boat, and struck up a deal. At the end of the month, we had our guys move the boat to the restaurant by the name of Las Jaibas. We were much happier in this new location and so were our guys, meaning the captain and first mate. The owner was also willing to allow us to use his restaurant for a little continental breakfast that we wanted to serve our clients. When we had gone down as tourists, we had a heck of a time finding a cup of coffee in the morning before we would go out on a tour. We wanted to offer our clientele something that no other boat company offered down there. You see, we did not know anything about boats, but we did know what it was like to be a tourist and what was missing from the other companies. We also decided that we were going to be there in the morning to greet our customers, serve them breakfast, talk to them, let them know what was going on, and send them on their way. We were also going to greet the boat as it came in from the tour and talk to the people and find out how everything went and make sure they were happy. If not, why? These were some of the services that we found lacking down there. You would never get to meet the owners of any business nor would anyone let you know what was going on, especially if there was a delay for any reason. We knew what we would have to offer would be a great thing. The main problem was getting the word out there so that people would find out about us.

Throughout all of the first summer there, the kids were trying to cope with a new place to live, new and different cultures to deal with, and of course, a new language. Trenton was and still is a very outgoing person, and we always felt that he would not have a difficult time getting to know other kids and neighbors. We were right; if we wanted to know anything about anybody in the neighborhood, all we had to do was ask Trenton. He would always know what was going on. He was out and about the neighborhood and beyond almost as soon as we moved in. He used to ride around with the coco frío man on his little cart made from an old bicycle. Every day there are people driving, riding their bicycle carts, or walking up and down the streets selling their wares. Be it the gas truck with tanks of gas for cooking and heating water, bottled water in garrafóns, bread and sweet bread, coco frío, or homemade food, you could get just about anything you needed without leaving the house. Everyone has their own special noise that they make so that you know that they are coming and can run out if that is what you want to buy. You do not have to look to see who it is; you just know the sounds that they make. Besides the wares, you also have people that do yard work, shoe repair guys, and people that sharpen blades like for a machete. Almost everything that your heart desires is there right at your beck and call. It is really neat, and a very different way of living than the one that most Americans are used to.

Trenton and Brittnay were learning the language much faster than Laurel and I. Brittnay had met a boy that she was very attracted to. He spoke absolutely no English, so this made her learn Spanish all the faster. Trenton was out every day playing with the kids, so he too learned Spanish rapidly. Not only did they learn it, but they learned to speak it with the Yucatán accent that is very prevalent in Cancun. Laurel and I eventually spoke with the same accent. School starts at about the middle of August in Mexico. Laurel had enrolled Brittnay into the American school and was paying $300 a month for Brittnay to attend this school. Trenton, however, was not being permitted to enter his grade because it was taught 80 percent in Spanish, and he did not speak enough Spanish at that time. They would have allowed him to repeat the fifth grade for $300 a month even though Laurel had previously been told that both kids would have no problems with going to school down there. This meant that Brittnay was going to be going to school, and Trenton was going to have to take a year off to learn Spanish. This also meant that Trenton was going to be going with us everywhere, learning the business from the ground up. We felt very bad about this, but there was nothing that could be done. We were committed to this thing by then, and that was how it was going to have to be. Trenton went with us to the harbor master's office, which was almost an everyday occurrence.

August rolled around, and Brittnay started school. She had her own private Spanish class since she was the only child in school that did not already speak Spanish. She had this class four hours a week, so it was pretty intense learning. She not only was learning to speak Spanish, but she also learned to read, spell, and do proper grammar. Too bad that Laurel and I could not have learned right along with her, but we had our own problems to deal with. We were still trying to acquire our permits. We were still running to the harbor master's office almost every day. Poor Charlie, our marketing man, was trying to market a product that we had no idea when it would be available to sell. He got a big offer (it was big to us at that time) from LaBoom to advertise through them. They have promotions and giveaways a couple of times a week. Charlie got us in the door there, and they were going to be giving away free trips on our boat as a prize. We were also given permission to advertise on their busses, and we could have put big signs on the sides of their busses when the time came. However, we were never able to afford anything on that grand of a scale.

In September, Laurel had been in the hotel zone, working on something or another, and her car broke down. She had to park it, find a phone, and call me to come and get her. While she was waiting for me to get there, she decided to go to one of the bars on the street, sit and wait for me there, and have a beer. As fate would have it, she met the man of her dreams whose name is Lalo. *Lalo* is short for "Eduardo." Almost everyone has a nickname or a little name that is short for a longer name. For instance, the name *Pancho* is short for "Francisco." Lalo is a waiter in the hotel zone. Many of the waiters there went to school to be doctors, teachers, lawyers, etcetera. However, they are able to make more money as a waiter, so that is what they do when they are young. When they get too old to be waiters, then they go and work at their professional field.

We finally received our last permit the middle of November. We were so very overjoyed, I cannot tell you the elation there was between us. However, that was not to last too long. Right after we finally got our last permit, we had to deal with our first hurricane. I do not know if you have ever been near the ocean when a hurricane is coming, but it is very eerie. We were basically instructed by our captain what we needed to do. We had to go and buy food supplies for them and water of course. They needed extra gas, ropes, flashlights, etcetera. When there is a hurricane coming down there, all the boats that can get through to the lagoon side go into the lagoon area and tie up into the mangroves. They also tie up to big palm trees that are growing on the sides of the road or basically anything that would help to keep a boat safe. The boats that cannot get into the lagoon, such as sail boats with masts sticking up, go over to Isla Mujeres. At Isla Mujeres, there is a lagoon-type area behind tall rocky cliffs that are out on the Caribbean. These are at the southern part of the island, and all the boats go into this area, tie up to each other and the mangroves, and sit it out. The captains of the boats and mates go over also and stay there with the boats. This is what we were told that needed to be done. So the day before the hurricane was supposed to hit, we stood on the dock and watched our boat and our guys sail away over to the island. What a feeling. These men leave their wives, children, houses, everything and go with the boat. We could not believe it. God was good to us, and the hurricane ended up to be only a category one.

After it was all over with and the rain had stopped, Kevin called us and wanted us to come and pick him up so that he could take us down town in my truck and show us what the streets were like. We got over on Portillo down in the lower areas, and there were kids swimming in the streets. Now this is not clean rainwater that they were playing in; this is water that has been lying in the streets along with the sewers that overflow along with the rainwater. Whenever it would rain there for at least half an hour or so, the streets would flood because of the poor sewer systems. At those times, it was good to have my truck to drive, believe me. Some of the stores along Portillo were all flooded out, but of course, it could have been a lot worse.

When the waters calmed down and the port was opened back up, the guys were then allowed to bring the boat back. What a welcome site to see—the guys and the boat all in one piece and safe! A couple of weeks later, the whole scenario took place again. Once again, it was another category one. By the end of November, we were finally ready to start our tour business for real. Charlie went around, and Laurel and I did also, telling all the personal concierges that we were ready to be up and running. Laurel and I had purchased a big coffee pot from Sam's Club for all our customers that we were going to have. We waited and waited and waited for our first tour. We revisited the personal concierges several times and still waited. In December, our captain had been in the hotel zone for some unknown reason and ran into an American man and was talking to him. While he was talking to him, our boat tour came up in the conversation. Lo and behold, our captain actually was responsible for our first tour. The tour was a private tour, no less, which is always a plus. The people were from California, and they not only were our first customers, but they went out on our boat as a private tour every time that they came down to Cancun. What nice people they were, and we will never forget them. That was our beginning of tours.

Trenton Meets D.I.F.

O ne day in the first six to eight months of living in Cancun, Laurel and I were on our way out to Bonfil to get some boat supplies. Bonfil is a little town that you pass through on your way out to the airport, if you have been to Cancun. Laurel received a phone call from Trenton. A *very* frantic Trenton was screaming that he was going to be taken away from us! He had been in the Mercado Veinte ocho or Market 28, if you have ever been there shopping. He could not go to school, as you might remember, so he was going there because it was quite close to where Laurel was living at that time, and he would work for his friend's dad who had a store there. Trenton was and is a very good salesman. Even at his ripe young age of eleven or twelve, he could sell you just about anything.

The other store owners did not like the fact that he was working there and pulling in American customers left and right. They accused him of pulling in customers from their stores and called an organization down there called DIF. It is an organization for the protection of children. After hearing Trenton screaming and crying on the phone, a man came on the phone and told Laurel that her son was being taken away out of the market place and down to their place. She was telling him that they had better not touch her son and that she would be right there! We turned the car around as soon as we could and started heading back into Cancun.

We spotted a truck that we thought belonged to our friend Carlos, the guy that had delivered our boat for us. We caught up to him, and sure enough, it was him! We yelled in his window that we needed his help and could he follow us. He said that he could and did. We drove directly to Mercado Veinte ocho and parked the car. We caught up with Carlos and started walking to the store where we figured Trenton would be. Well, there was no doubt where he was. When we got around that area, there were about one hundred people all standing around, watching. There were several police officers and around six DIF officers. Two were holding Trenton, one by each arm, preventing him from running to us. He started screaming, "Let me go. Let me go," and he was crying. They would not let him go until we got right up to him. We were very upset to say the least!

Carlos immediately started talking to the guys, and in fact, he knew some of them. Of course everyone was still standing around, watching. Finally, Carlos was able to make them listen and got them all calmed down and explained to them who we were, what we were doing in Cancun, and why Trenton was not in school. Trenton and we were informed that Trenton was no longer allowed into the Market 28 alone without an adult with him. He was no longer going to be allowed to work there or anywhere else. So that was the end of his working in Mercado Veinte ocho. What a scare he and we had that day! Once again, thank God for Carlos, and thank God for sending him on the same road that we were traveling at the same time. It was just another time when God chose to remain anonymous.

Christmas of 2002

Soon, Christmas was upon us. We were all still living together at this time, but things were getting a little sticky with all of us in the same household. Laurel really wanted a Christmas tree and said that she would buy one. Yes, they do have real evergreen trees for Christmas. We would go to a grocery store or to Walmart, and the smell of those trees would be over whelming. It was always a reminder of home back in Michigan. We always went to a tree farm to cut our own Christmas tree every year. It was a great tradition and great fun searching for just the right tree. Usually, at that time of year, we were tromping through snow and, sometimes, quite a bit of it. When there is a lot of snow, it is sometimes difficult to actually see the tree and the would-be bare spots. When the perfect tree was found after checking out many, many trees, then we would cut it down, drag it out to the place to pay for it, put it in the truck, and take it home with pride. Therefore, a real, live Christmas tree was a very important item for all of us at Christmas. Laurel and the kids went and purchased a tree.

Our 1ˢᵗ Christmas tree in Cancun. This is Brittnay.

All of the trees down there come with two pieces of wood crisscrossed and nailed to the bottom of the tree. That was the standard. The tree was never put in water, so you can imagine what it started looking like in the house after awhile in that heat! Kind of like a Charlie Brown Christmas tree. When we weren't sweeping up dog hair, we were sweeping up tree needles or both! We decorated the tree; Laurel had brought her decorations down with her. However, by this time, money was running out, so there were not many presents under that tree. By Christmas, all of Trenton's things that he had brought down—skateboard and rollerblades—had since been stolen because he had left them outside in our yard. Along with all those, our bikes had been stolen also. The first time that we forgot to lock the gate at night, it was like whoever took them was going by every night to see if we had locked up or not. We were not used to locking anything up, having come from country living. I live on a private drive, and hardly any people that I do not know are around at any time. Therefore, we were not used to locking anything up. Live and learn! Laurel bought Trenton a new bike and some socks for Christmas. That was pretty much it. I had bought some summer things that were on sale when I had gone back to the states in September for a month. I flew back specifically to go trail riding on my horse with my girlfriends and also went to Quarter Horse Congress that year with them.

We wanted to do something for our employees for Christmas besides, giving them their aguinaldo, which is their Christmas bonus, and it consists of the amount of their salary and has to be paid by December 20. We invited them over for dinner along with their families. Cesar was not married and came alone, but Pablo brought his fiancé with him, and Charlie also brought his fiancé. We grilled steaks out on the grill and had the trimmings, and I also baked apple pies. I am known for my pies, especially the crust. So that is what we did for them. After the dinner, when everyone left, we asked Charlie to stay so that we could talk to him. We had decided that we had to let him go. We could no longer afford to pay his salary. When we told him, we both were crying; that is how badly we felt. We kept him on as our partner, and actually, things did work out for the best for him not working for us. He eventually got married; he and his wife moved to Cabo San Lucas where she was sent for her job. They are now back in Cancun and have a baby.

Laurel, right before and during Christmas, came down with typhoid fever and another fever. She was so deathly ill, I thought that she was going to die. We finally took her to the hospital to have her checked out. They diagnosed her and gave her medications to take, and she came back home to be nursed back to health. Thank God she did survive, but it surely was a touch-and-go situation for quite a while. I was so worried about her, and thankfully, she pulled through. We certainly began to learn what were the important things in life, and they sure weren't things as most of us here in America have come to believe. Shortly after Christmas, Laurel and the kids moved into a house that Lalo was living in that actually belonged to his father. However, his parents did not live there; they lived in Merida. It started to become apparent to Laurel that I needed some space when I started locking myself in my upstairs bedroom when we were home. It was getting very difficult for all of us to be all living together. I am a neat freak, and Laurel and her children are completely the opposite. Sometimes, closeness can become stifling on both sides, and it was time!

Laurel Gets Her Own Place

L aurel left her rescue puppy with me, whose name was LaBats because we thought it would be cute since Kevin had a dog named Molsen. She was about three or four months old when they moved, and it was just easier to leave her with Fargo and me. In the evenings, I would take both dogs walking with me. We would go for miles and miles. I never ever feared for myself probably because I had Fargo. He weighed 130 lbs. when we moved down there. He had lost probably around 10 lbs. when he was so sick. I had no TV and no radio to listen to, so I either read books or went walking. Sometimes, I would get a little lost, but I always found my way back to the house. One evening, I did have to ask where my street or the nearest large cross street was. I was able to speak enough Spanish by then to be able to ask and understand the answer. There was a jungle and park on Kabah, which was a four-lane street pretty close to my house. I used to walk there because I could let the dogs off leash and let them run. They really enjoyed that part of the walk the most. Then there was a place to go across Kabah where they had put streets in and were getting ready to build houses. That went on for miles and miles also. There were always construction guys working or bedding down for the night. When there is construction going on, a lot of the guys stay at the construction site overnight to protect the building materials that are left to work with—materials such as cement blocks, sand and stone, and bags of cement to mix the mortar to build. They cook right there, build tar paper huts, and hang their hammocks, and they are good for the night. I, once again, never had fear of walking down those desolate areas because I had Fargo. I was very fortunate that nothing ever happen.

After the private tour, we thought we were on our way, but we still waited and waited. We finally started talking about going to some of the travel agencies and signing contracts. The first one we went to was Olympus tours. They pretended to be interested and told us to come back for a second appointment with a manager higher-up, but when we did, he absolutely refused to offer us a contract. The same thing happened with Lomus Travel, Caribe, and IMS Travel. Well, never in our wildest dreams did we think that would happen. The problem was they were all so nice and all said, "Sure, we would love to sell your tour." Then they would just never talk with us again, or finally, they would tell us they could not because they had exclusive contracts with other marinas. We could not believe, after all the work and everything we had been through, that we were not going to make it.

One day, Kevin talked with us and told us about a company called the Royal Resorts. They were a time-share company with their own travel agency, Thomas Moore, inside each resort, and Kevin had a friend who was a manger in the travel agency. He set up a meeting for us and told us we would have to go in and sell our tour. The day came, and we went in very nervous. We met with a man called Ricardo Rodriguez, and after about twenty minutes or so, we liked him so much, and apparently, he really liked us too because he put our contract through to his boss with his recommendation, and they very reluctantly agreed to sign on with us! We had to supply them with a detailed description of our tour, what sort of breakfast we would have, what the people would be doing on our boat, pictures of our boat, a copy of insurance for the boat and passengers, detailed time frame of the tour, and if there was going to be transportation to and from the boat from the five resorts. *Yeah!* We were in like Flynn! Now for sure the people were going to start flocking out to be on our boat!

We went to all five of the resorts and visited all the Thomas Moore reps, introducing ourselves and explaining about our new tour. Laurel and I did this two or three times a week. We started to really know the reps, and after about a month, one of the reps, Alondra, from the Royal Sands sent us four people for our all-day island tour. The people returned after the tour and raved to Alondra about what a good time that they had. After their comments, she sent us more people. Then shortly after that, we had another rep call us with a reservation. When that group returned with great comments, we then began to get more and more reservations. Of course, Laurel and I were still going to visit them all every week. Things were beginning to take shape, and there was, once again, hope for the future.

Laurel and I never dreamed that things would be such a struggle. Through all the struggles, we became better Christians. We were both now reading the Bible more than ever before. Our faith in the Lord was being tested daily it seemed, and we were, for the most part, standing strong. Easter of 2003 was upon us. We wanted desperately to go to church. I am Lutheran by faith, but we ended up going to a Catholic church for Easter. We went to the open-air church by the Parque de Palapas off Tulum Avenue. We were lucky to get a seat toward the front of the church, and as soon as the music started playing and the singing began, I started bawling. I sat and cried throughout the entire service. All of the little children were looking at me, probably wondering what in the world was wrong with the gringa.

We did not understand the service, but we really enjoyed it. It meant a lot to us just to be able to be in church. Shortly after Easter, Laurel had to pull Brittnay out of school. She was not doing well at all, not studying, and Laurel was running out of money. Brittnay ran away from home, and she was gone for eight days before we were able to locate her. Let me tell you what a horrifying experience that was for all of us! All I could think of was that she had been kidnapped by some guy and that she was locked up somewhere being used as a sex slave or being sold for sexual favors. Laurel and I went out at night, searching for her after working all day with the boat. We went to the hotel zone where all the bars are and searched the bars. We talked with her friends that we knew and had them looking for her also. Of course, no one would tell us where she was even if they knew! We did not get much sleep and had to run the business during the day. We were just getting started and could not just close the shop. When we were around our clients, we had to pretend that everything was just great. You cannot imagine unless you have been through something similar what that was like. She finally turned up after eight days. What a joyous feeling that was to have her back alive and well. The feeling did not last too long, however, because she decided to move out with her boyfriend, Freddie. She was only fifteen years old at that time and would not be sixteen until June. She thought that she was in love, and you could not reason with her. She just kept telling us that she did not want the same things in life that we wanted such as a good education, good job, nice house, nice car, etcetera.

She ended up living right downtown where you do not wander out at night unescorted. They were living as the typical poor Mexican do in a rented one-room, no-kitchen, shared-bathroom, hammock-for a-bed-and-furniture, no-cooking-facilities place, nothing. She had to hand washthe clothes, and when she hung them out on the clothesline, she did not have clothes pins. What they do is untwist the clothes line and twist in the clothes. That is how they are hung out. If you are lucky, they are not stolen while they are hanging out. This is what she thought at the time was her little piece of heaven because she was living with her boyfriend and they were together. He worked at a bar as a waiter at night. A lot of the times, she would go to work with him and just sit there, waiting for him to get out of work. What a life! Laurel finally convinced her to come back to the house to live. In August, Laurel enrolled her in public high school, and we thought that things were going to get better. Well, she had met another loser when she was working at a restaurant in the hotel zone while living with Freddie. They were actually friends and kind of all hung out together. When Brittnay moved back with Laurel, she started dating this new guy, Dexter. By now, she was sixteen years old. She registered for school and started going, but that did not last very long. Two weeks after she moved back in with Laurel, she moved out again, this time with Dexter. Once again, they were living in a one-room cell.

In June of that year, I needed to find a less expensive house to rent since I was living alone and paying the whole amount of rent. Once again, the good Lord provided me with an excellent place. Laurel and I were visiting one of the hotels to see if their personal concierge had any questions about our tour or had anyone that was interested, and I just happened to have a newspaper on the dashboard open to houses for rent. The bellboy that we had talked to about leaving our car parked in front of the hotel while we ran in asked me if I was looking for a house to rent when we came back out from the hotel. I said, "Yes, I am." He then told me that he had a new house in a very nice neighborhood that he wanted to rent out because he was not living there. We set up a time to go and see the house. He met me with his mom, and they showed us the house, which turned out to be very nice. It was the nicest that I had looked at, and the neighborhood looked very nice. It was a fairly new subdivision-type neighborhood with a park at the end of the dead-end street. The house had three bedrooms, a bath and a half, and a kitchen with a stove and cupboards (This might not sound exciting to you, but it is very hard to find a house with kitchen cupboards or a stove.), so I was really excited about those features. The bedrooms, however, did not have any closets in them. The owner promised to have a closet built if I rented the house. It had a little walled in backyard, and I say *yard* for a lack of anything else to call it. Actually, it was a walled area with white coral, no grass, and clotheslines to dry the clothes, which is great for me. I decided on the spot to take it.

Shortly after I moved in, I went back to the states for a month to go trail riding with my friends once again and spend time with my horse, horse friends, family, and just be back. My girlfriend Karen, who keeps my horse for me, and I did a lot of riding together. I was able to stay with her daughter, Leslie, who lives right down the road from her mother's house about a mile away. Leslie is a single gal and a police officer, and she also trains and shows her horses in reining. She is hardly ever home, so that was a good place for me to be able to stay. We hardly ever saw each other, so I did not get on her nerves. You know how it is when you live alone; you are just used to your own private space. Every time that I went back to the states, I always stayed at Leslie's house. Another horse girlfriend of mine, Judy, has an old pickup truck that she only uses for hauling hay, grain, sawdust, etcetera. She always let me use her truck when I went back also, so I always had wheels when I went back. My friends were absolutely wonderful to me, and I do not know what I would have done without all their help. Michigan has a horse trail that goes all the way across the state and also cuts up the middle and goes to the Mackinaw Bridge area. On the trail about every twenty-five to thirty miles, there are campsites for you to haul your horse trailer up and leave it parked while you ride. You can stay overnight if you wish. They all have outdoor bathrooms and a pump for drinking water. This is my most favorite thing to do in the whole world; there is nothing like it as far as I am concerned. I was very fortunate to be able to come back and do the thing that I loved the most. I went back again in August or September to do some fall riding. Some of the things that I missed desperately were the color changes and the fresh smells.

We were really starting to get busy with the Royal Resorts, not as busy as we would have liked to be, but if it were not for paying a van service, we probably would have been able to make a little money. Laurel and I were still not receiving any money such as payroll from the business. However, in October of 2003, we had the boat pulled out over at Isla Mujeres to have some fiberglass work done, a hole patched that was in the bottom of one of the hauls that we did not know about when we bought the boat, and had it repainted. Isla Mujeres is the only boat yard in and around Cancun. So if you need to have your boat pulled out of the water, that is where you have to take it. We were quoted a price to pull it out, so much per day for sitting there and putting it back in when finished. Our captain had a "friend" who did fiberglass work and also painted. We trusted our captain, so we went with this guy. The captain also went with me to various places to buy all the materials that would be needed to repair the boat, paint it, etcetera. After the boat was pulled out, the captain of the port or harbor master on Isla Mujeres sent one of his guys down to the marina to inform me that I needed to go to the harbor master's office on the island and pay a fee for pulling the boat out. There is a fee that we had to pay because our boat is a tourist boat. It was not a cheep fee either; it ran around US $250. I had to go to the bank on the island to the ATM machine and pull the money from my savings account back in the States to take care of this. So on with the repair work.

I drove my truck to the car ferry loaded with supplies that I had just purchased; we took the ferry across to the island, and I then drove to the marina. Laurel and I thought this was pretty cool to be driving on the same island where we had been as tourists. Who would have thought that we one day would be driving our own vehicle on that very same island! It was like a dream. In fact, every time we sent the boat out with tourists, we had to pinch each other to make sure that we were not dreaming. What was only going to take two weeks ended up taking three weeks. They tore all of the old foam out of the boat and the rotten wood. They reconstructed the whole inside and fiber glassed inside and out. Our colors for our company were pink and purple. Our website colors were pink and purple as were our uniforms. However, we did not make our guys wear pink. They wore white polo shirts and tan shorts. We also wore these colors until later when we had purple polo shirts made. We had pink and purple paint mixed to paint the outside of the boat.

While the boat was on the island, Laurel or I or both of us would go over there occasionally to see how the guys were doing. We were really not happy with the way things were or were not proceeding. One day I went there, and there was no one there! They gave me the excuse that it had been raining early that morning, so they did not go. We were paying for the ferry to get to the island and the ferry to get back. They also expected us to pay for their food while they were working on the island. I kept telling them to pack a lunch. This is unheard of there for that type of worker. They do not ordinarily eat sandwiches for lunch; they ate chicken, rice, tortillas, beans, etcetera . So for me to tell them to bring their lunch was I guess insulting to them. I kept telling them that in the United States, the construction workers all bring their own lunch and that is what I expected them to do. This did not go over really well, but I did not give into their requests. After all, we were paying them double what any other boat company was paying at that time. Also, when we did not have a tour, we did not make our guys come into work. They sat home on their —— and got paid. That was highly unusual also. You either worked, or you did not get paid. When I got back from the island, I called Laurel and told her what I had found—no one working on the boat! The next day, we both went over to the island early in the morning. They were all there; the two that we had hired to do the work on the boat and Pablo were hard at work. The captain, Cesar, however was not doing anything as usual. Laurel got into it with him about not being there the day before, and he, of course, was arguing back. It is very hard to get the respect as a boss that a man would automatically get just by being a man. In the end, Cesar told us that he quit, climbed into the boat, and took the bitácora. This is an empty record book that we had to take to the harbor master, and he then puts his original stamp on each blank page. The captain then records every day-to-day happening on the boat in this book such as the weather, anything that is wrong and needs fixing on the boat, what took place during the tour, what time the boat left the dock, what time they arrived at the end of the day, etcetera. The book belongs to the boat and owners of the boat. Cesar tried to tell us that the book was his and that he was taking it with him! He went ballistic, and this was the first time that we had seen this side of him. We finally managed to smooth things out because all I could think of was that our boat was over here in dry dock. Once it was ready to be launched again, who would we get for a captain to bring it back to Cancun?

It came time to start painting the boat, and both Laurel and I wanted to be there to see the color go on. We were very excited to finally get our boat painted the colors that we had wanted ever since we bought the boat. When she was finally all done, she was so beautiful. We were two happy campers; that is for sure. The day that we had planned on launching the boat and taking it back over to Cancun to Las Jaibas was very windy. We went over to the island and paid our bill. We were unable to sail back with the boat, however, because of the strong north winds. The harbor master gave his permission for the captain to sail the boat over, but we could not be on the boat. We got back to Las Jaibas, and the longer we waited, the stronger the wind became. We finally decided that the captain should leave the boat there overnight and try again the next day. However, when we called him to tell him to leave the boat there, he was already on his way. We waited and waited for him. We finally got a frantic call from him that the motor had stopped, and he could not get it started again. In the meantime, he was being blown way off course. We started driving north toward Punta Sam. Sure enough, that is where we finally found our boat, stuck in the sand with the brand-new paint job on the rudders and the repair work that had been done to the rudders being jeopardized as well. We were not happy campers any longer!

We had to drive down to Las Jaibas and ask the owner if he would go and tow our boat back to the dock with his fishing boat. He did, and that is how we got our boat back to the dock. The paint color lasted approximately a grand total of two weeks. The pink then turned white, and the purple turned blue. Unbeknownst to us at that time and for some time later, the guys used car paint instead of boat paint. The bottom paint lasted not quite a year. I had bought the bottom paint myself from a guy on the island that sold boat supplies. I thought I was getting a good deal, but as it turned out once again, he was the one getting the deal!

Trenton

Trenton by now was finally in school. He had become very fluent in Spanish. In fact, you could not tell him from any other Mexican speaking the language. Laurel enrolled him in public school close to the house where they were living. He was the only gringo in the whole school, and he now had to learn to read and write in Spanish. That was a struggle, but thank God; he provided Trenton with an excellent, caring teacher. In the public schools, if the teacher does not show up for work that day, there is no one to teach the kids; they are just there doing whatever. This situation happens quite often, unfortunately, but Trenton's teacher was an exception to the rule. She would also sit right next to Trenton when he had to take a test and read for him in Spanish to try and help him get through. She was a wonderful person and really helped him a great deal. He is the type of person that loves attention, so that was right up his alley! By Christmas time, he was well adjusted to going to public school, got along with all the kids, and learned how to read and write in Spanish. It has since become his first language because he was so young when we moved. He is now learning everything in Spanish, and a lot of the things he is learning, he does not know how to say in English (like science for instance).

Throughout the entire time of us having and running the business, Trenton was a great help to us. He was also, don't get me wrong, trouble at times. I know it was a rough adjustment for him and took him sometime to realize or find his niche in the whole scheme of things down there. You know how hard boys can be on one another, and then he had to try to fit in being more or less the only gringo around. This is because we lived in the real world not in a world where you move somewhere foreign, form your own little community of Americans, and carry on as usual. We did not have the money nor the desire to live this way. We wanted to fit in and learn the language and experience everything that we possibly could of living in a foreign land. Believe me, we did just that and more!

Six weeks before Easter, as in New Orleans, they have Mardi Gras. They refer to it as Carnival. They have parades with large floats; each school participates in the parades, and each school elects a king and queen of the Carnival. Trenton was voted king of the Carnival for his school. They have a big crowning ceremony at the school in the evening, and all the parents were invited. It is a very big deal, and of course, we went. Of course, we were the only gringas there. There was no problem telling who his family was! We went to the parade that Trenton was in, and he danced the whole time behind the float. Our little star was on the Televista. That is how well he was accepted by the other children in his school. Maybe we could all take a lesson from the children. We were very proud of him, and the whole Carnival was a great experience.

Christmas of 2003 was pretty much nondescript as far as Christmases had gone for us in the past. We went to the Catholic church in the Parque de Palapas once again. However, it was so full by the time we got there, we had to stand outside and try to hear and understand. I do not know what was more difficult at that time, the hearing or the understanding. At that point in time, it was probably the understanding. We were not that fluent in Spanish yet. I had purchased summer sale items once again when I had been back to Michigan in the fall for everyone. That was pretty much our Christmas. We had Christmas dinner, and we were together, and we had our faith in our Lord. That, we were learning, was the most important thing. It is not about what who got who or who got what. We both had a house to live in, and we had food on our table every day. That was our blessings, and we were thankful for them and thankful for our faith in the Lord.

Shortly after Christmas, I had a very surprising evening take place. Do you remember me telling you about Palemon? This is the captain that we had wanted to work for us at the beginning. I arrived at work (the dock) one fine day, and there sat Palemon. We greeted each other and chitchatted for a bit, and then he asked me if we were still looking for a captain and that he was available for us. He had quit his job at the big boat company which was our competition. I told him no and that we had a captain and that we were happy with him. He gave me his cell phone number and told me that if I should hear of anyone looking for a captain to let him know. I told him that I certainly would do that, not telling him that no one in the boat world down there talked to us. We would be the last to know anything that was going on down there as far as the boat business was concerned if they had it their way. He left, and I felt bad that we could not hire him on the spot. We were not that kind of people and would not fire someone just to hire someone else. I was happy with Cesar; he had become like a friend as both the guys by then seemed to us. I often times picked up Cesar and took him to work in the morning. When I was looking for a different house to move to, he had helped me look. I was the one that went downtown where all the *taller* shops were where they repaired anything that you needed repairing. So in our travels, we would of course talk with each other about things that friends talk about.

This telling you of Cesar and how he helped me reminds me of the whole "we need to change the way that the catamaran is steered" story. When Cesar became captain, one of the first things that he wanted changed on our boat was the steering. He took me to a metal repair shop on Routo Quatro and introduced me to the owner. Of course, English was never spoken at any of these tallers; they always only spoke Spanish. Among the three, they redesigned the steering system on the boat and I paid.

Imagine that! It did seem to make sense, and it seemed to make our captain happier with the way the boat was handled when all was said and done. That was the important thing to us—make everything perfect on the boat so there would be no problems.

In January of 2004, things started to pick up more. The first two weeks of January are pretty slow as far as tourism goes. Then things start picking up. As tourism picks up, however, so do the north winds. North winds to us were very troublesome indeed. When we have north winds, they often times make the seas too rough to run tours. When this would happen, we would have to cancel our tours. We not only would have to cancel the tour but do so in a timely manner so that our vans did not pick up our people and bring them out to the boat. This was a big inconvenience to our clients who would have their entire day planned with us, come out to the boat, and then not be able to go out on the tour as planned. This not only was an inconvenience to our clients; it was very expensive for us as well. Laurel and I both would lie awake in the middle of the night listening to the winds. I had chimes on the north side of my house, and they were right by my bedroom window. Therefore, when the winds were blowing from the north, I could wake up and hear my chimes. Then we would lie awake worrying whether we would have a tour the next day. We had a system worked out with Cesar, our captain. He would go out to the boat early and call on our marine radio to the harbor master to ask if the port was open or closed. If it was closed, he was to call us and let us know. Based on this information, we would call the Royal Resorts and cancel the tour.

One morning, after dealing with the port being closed day after day after day and canceling tours one after another, we went out to the boat knowing that the port was not closed because we did not hear from Cesar. Laurel and I arrived and started unloading everything that we needed for the continental breakfast. Before the tours every morning, we would have to go and buy sweet bread or, as you would know it, breakfast rolls, doughnuts, ice for the coolers, etcetera. If the tour was not an all day island tour but only the four hour sailing/snorkeling tour, I also had to make the snacks that were served on the boat which usually were ham and cheese croissants or sandwiches made from French bread. Cesar met us at the door of the restaurant and proceeded to tell us that the port was closed. We were dumfounded to say the least! Laurel started asking Cesar why he had not let us know ahead of time, and he just went ballistic! He hit her and shoved her out of the restaurant and told her that she was in his country and he could do anything that he wanted!

The day before had been the "quincena", which is payday. Mostly everyone down there gets paid every fifteen days. Well, that was the day before the port was closed, so the guys did not have to show up at work. That is another thing that we did for our employees that no other boat company did. When the port was closed and if they had all their work done on the boat such as cleaning and little repairs, they did not have to be at work, and we paid them. This was established around the previous November when the port was closed quite a bit also. One day, Pablo presented me with a letter basically stating that he did not understand why they had to show up at work day after day when the port was closed basically doing nothing. He wanted that changed, or he was going to quit. The letter was written in English the best that his wife could do, but we really did not understand it. So once again, we called our dear friend Kevin to come out to the boat dock and talk with Pablo to find out what exactly the major problem was. So we then, at that time, changed our policy to where they did not have to come in when the port was closed, but they still received their full pay. The only thing they did not make was tips.

After the fiasco at the restaurant and while Laurel was outside trying to get a hold of the Royal Resorts and the van service to cancel everything, I was inside paying the guys. That was me! The peacemaker and very naive! I wanted to always be fair!

Cesar left the restaurant, and unbeknownst to us had taken all the legal papers off the boat from the harbor master. A copy of all our permits had to be kept on the boat at all times in case it was stopped at the island or in the waters. This was done quite regularly because a lot of the boat companies down there run tourists without their permits. They pay a fine and go on their merry way until the next time. Anyway, he took all those permits plus the bitácora. When he left the marina, we found out a little later, he ran right to the court system and filed a complaint against us, which is called a demanda. He stated that we fired him for no reason and that we swore at him. Needless to say, we ended up having to hire an attorney; Laurel went to court because I just could not deal with the whole situation. I felt very betrayed and hurt and angry, and I did not know what would happen to me physically if I went into that court room. So I stayed away. This was a long process, probably taking about six months to resolve. It ended up costing us a whole bunch of money for an attorney, and we ended up having to pay Cesar around $1,200.

After he quit, I called Palemon to see if he was currently employed. He told me that he was working at the present time. However, he was driving a taxi and that he had just gotten in an accident about half an hour prior to my phone call. I told him that I was looking for a captain and wanted to know if he was interested. He said, "Yes, when do you want me to start?" I told him tomorrow, and he said, "I will be there." That is how we got our Palemon as our captain. God does work in mysterious ways, doesn't he? How did Palemon end up driving a taxi, you are probably wondering. When I had talked to him out on the dock that day he was asking for a job, he told me that he was thinking of driving a taxi. He said that he knew some people that were making a lot of money driving taxis. The man had never driven a car in his entire life! He went to to his brother-in-law's house, drove his car for three days, came back to Cancun, and passed the taxi driving test and became a taxicab driver. If you have ever been to Cancun and watched the taxis or the busses, you will surely know that this story is not an exaggeration. I could just never imagine this man driving a car on the hot, steamy streets of Cancun, with no air-conditioning, noise of horns honking, traffic noise, etcetera, for a living. This is a man who had been sailing the Caribbean where there is usually a nice breeze, where the water is beautiful, where it is reasonably peaceful most of the time, and where he was a captain of a boat; he had grown up on the seas as his father was a fisherman. It just did not fit! He was very glad to get back on a boat in the Caribbean as opposed to driving in the crazy traffic of Cancun. Things were looking up for us. We were getting busy, and we had the captain that we had always wanted from the beginning; life was good.

Brittnay

We were not seeing much of Brittnay these days. We did, however, see her at Easter time. When she came to the house, Laurel and I both noticed various bruises on her. We asked her about them and of course got the typical answers that someone who is being physically abused gives. We decided to plan a women's day and told her about it and that we expected her to come. We made arrangements to meet her on Tulum Avenue near the Burger King. Laurel and I arrived a little early and half-expected Britt not to show. However, she did, hand in hand with Dexter at her side. We got her away and spent the whole day together. I had told Laurel that she had to let Brittnay know that if she needed an out, she had a place to come. Laurel did this on the way, taking Brittnay to where she was living. However, Brittnay asked Laurel not to take her there but take her to the house of Dexter's mother. Brittnay knew that if she went to the place that they were living in together, she would get the s——— beat out of her.

The next morning, Laurel got a phone call. It was Brittnay asking to be picked up. Laurel went and got her before the boat went out. Thanks be to God, the port was closed that day. Laurel and Brittnay arrived a little later than I, and they were both crying. Laurel got out of the car and briefly told me that when Dexter had gotten to his mother's house; he went up one side of Brittnay and down the other, calling her every name that you possible can imagine. This was done in front of his own mother! We got Palemon, our captain, and Pablo, our first mate, in my truck and headed for where she had been living to get her things.

As it turned out, they had been living in a back room belonging to his uncle. Everything was locked up; you see most people live behind bars—bars on the windows, bars on the doors, and bars in gates. This is what was present at this house when we arrived.

The uncle came out of the house but inside the gate. He stated that Dexter was not there and that he could not let Brittnay in to get her things. We stood out there and argued with him for quite some time and decided to call the police. That is when he let us through the gate. Laurel got back to the room that they had been living in, and there was a steel locked door. She pounded and pounded on it and finally started kicking it. She almost had the thing kicked in, and he started throwing Brittnay's clothes out the barred window. He was too cowardly to come out, which is probably a good thing because he would not be alive today. I stood out on the sidewalk holding Brittnay while she continued crying. We were just wishing that he would come out as our captain is not a weakling and our first mate was a very big guy. We had backup, not that Laurel would have needed it! Her adrenalin was flowing pretty good at that time. After we got Brittnay's things and were on our way away from there, we had to take the guys back to the boat. We then went to Laurel's house, and she told me that we had to get Brittnay out of Mexico and back to the States as soon as possible. I called my son, Mick, but he was not home. I did, however, get in contact with my daughter-in-law, Lisa, and told her what was going on with Brittnay. I asked if we could send Brittnay to them. She said, "Yes, send her." I asked if she wanted to ask Mick first, and she said, "No, she is family. Send her." I thought this was absolutely wonderful on her part. We got a ticket out of Cancun the very next day.

She lived with Mick and Lisa from April 2004 through July of 2004. She was unable to find work where they lived. They lived in a very little town in northern Michigan where tourism is a lot of the industry. She was sleeping in until 1:00 or 2:00 p.m. and staying up half of the night. It was very hard on their family as

Lisa had a daughter two years younger than Britt, and they had a six-year-old son, James. Laurel was financially unable to send them any monetary help as we were barely making it ourselves! Toward the end of her time with Mick, I had been talking with my niece Cathy, whom I have previously mentioned earlier in the book as one of my nieces that I helped raise. Cathy had moved down to Florida and started her own business about the same time that we had moved to Cancun. However, her business was doing well, and she said that Brittnay could come down and live with and work for her. This was great. Brittnay would be in weather that she preferred more so than Michigan, and she could work. She was with Cathy for August, September, and October of 2004.

When Cathy received her first phone bill for $750 because Brittnay had been calling that you-know-who in Cancun, she hit the roof! We could not believe it and wondered if she was ever going to learn! While Brittnay was at Cathy's house, Laurel had been searching the Internet for a place for this kid. What were we going to do with her, and what in the world was going to become of her? We thought of the service, but you had to be a college grad or student to get into the service at that time. What were we going to do?

One evening, Laurel discovered the Job Corps on the Internet. It sounded like the perfect solution to this problem. Brittnay had to agree to go and sign up and wanted to be in Florida. However, at that time, Florida had no openings. They found an opening for Brittnay in Kentucky but not right away. Cathy could no longer be responsible and had a deadline for her to be out of the house. Laurel had to fly to Florida and meet Brittnay and go to the Job Corp in Florida and sign up. Laurel had to sign papers allowing Brittnay to enter this program. There was going to be a two-week period that Brittnay would have nowhere to live. Cathy found a women's shelter in Florida for her to go and wait for an opening in the Kentucky program. She was there for two weeks; a plane ticket was purchased for her, and she was on her way to Kentucky. Brittnay was now seventeen years old. Wow! Only seventeen and she had already been through quite a bit with more to come!

This is a wonderful program for teens and young adults. They met her at the airport and took her right to the school. It is built like a college campus, more or less. You have no chances to screw up. If you do not make curfew, you are out. If you do not pass drug tests, you are out. If you are caught with alcohol, you are out. If you are caught fighting, you are out. Brittnay ended up in a very tough part of Kentucky where she ended up being the only white girl on the campus. She struggled at first, but slowly and surely, she made her way. She decided to go for her GED as opposed to her diploma. Laurel had told her that she could not return to Cancun without one of the two in her hand. Brittnay started studying, getting up early (that was a plus in itself), living by the rules, and succeeding! She became a floor monitor and was getting an education in business. She also was working and getting paid. What a terrific program! I had always thought that the Job Corps was similar to the Peace Corps for some reason probably because I never needed to know before this what the difference was. Brittnay was very lonely at Christmas and wrote this message to the family.

I quote it word for word:

> Well it is Christmas Eve Evening and the sky is dark blue… there is a light COLD breeze and the regular trees are slightly waving… Ok, ok ok, I'm not going to continue the same as my mother (Laurel had written a Christmas letter to the family that same morning which will be included at a later date in the book) it just sounded like a good start. Hehehehehehe…So it's about 3 degrees outside and I am snowed inside now for three days….This is how you know when you are in Kentucky…because they closed everything down for two feet of snow. Oh my goodness! They won't even let me go to church, that is how freaky the people are here. All they need is some salt and plows…Gee Wiz! I

have to admit it is nice having snow for Christmas again. The only thing is that I thought once it snowed, it would feel like Christmas; but how wrong I was!

It doesn't feel like Christmas not one bit. I have no family here, not even a single Christmas cookie. Poor me. Yeah, I miss Grandma's Christmas cookies and most of all I miss being able to be with my Mother and little Brother this Christmas. However, I look at it this way... God had other plans in his head when I came here. I want to let everybody know how well I'm doing here. I finally feel confident in how my future is going to turn out. I feel more secure and safe. Most of all, I have finally realized how important family is. I don't know what I would have done without all of you to be there for me. You all let me know that no matter what happens, I will always have family that loves me and will do anything for me. Thank you so much. I probably would have been dead by now if it wasn't for you all. The life I was leading was definitely the wrong one. It was all about alcohol and the so called love of my life...hahahahahaha and being on my own and being a woman.

Little did I know that that was not what a woman was. That was not what an adult was. That was not the life somebody intelligent (like me) would choose to live. I may not be a workman yet, but I am a lot closer to it now than I was before I came to Kentucky and joined the Job Corp. Here at the job Corp, I have gotten my GED and now I'm just training for a job of my choice. Business tech for all those who don't know. I am learning how to handle myself as a lady and as a woman. I'm learning how to deal with other people and to try and get a long with everybody. This was the best decision I have ever made in my entire life; and honestly, I am very proud of myself. I want to say thank you to my mama because if she hadn't told me about Job Corp, I wouldn't be here at this program. I would still be struggling. OK anyway, enough of my sappy thanks. I want to get back to what I wanted to say about Christmas.

In my Mother's e-mail she started to reflect on Christmas past. Everything she said about my papa, even though I was so little, honestly, I can still remember. I especially remember one Christmas not having anything to give him for Christmas. I tried making him a fishing pole out of paper and string...Hahahahahaha....I miss him greatly; and on the contrary, I think about him often. I never got the chance to really know him; but yet I still miss him greatly and love him with all my heart. As far as Aunt Jan goes, I can't remember. All I remember is going over to her house and watching Trent run around with one slipper on his foot...Hmmmm...Anyway, I wish everybody has a very Merry Christmas and a Happy New Year. Thank you, thank you, thank you for being my family!!! Crazy but loving...yes everybody in our family is psycotic! From Kentucky, weird but true...Britt.

It is amazing how she changed in such a short period. Well, maybe not changed but became her old self once again. Praise the Lord! Laurel and I both bawled our eyes out when we read this for the first time. It still makes my heart flutter to know what a wonderful granddaughter I have. God bless and keep you always in his arms, Britt.

This is a copy of Laurel's Christmas letter that she had written on the Christmas Eve morning, the letter that Brittnay was referring to in her letter:

Well, it is Christmas Eve morning here and the sky is a light blue. There is a light breeze and the palm trees are slightly waving. It will be around 80 degrees today and another beautiful day in paradise; and all I can think about is Michigan! There is nothing better than to have snow on Christmas, a fire in the fireplace and sweaters, jackets and boots. We know you have had a difficult winter so far, we always want what we don't have! Today and tomorrow enjoy the snow for us please.

There will just be the five of us for Christmas dinner this year. We are having dinner on Christmas eve as both of our boyfriends have to work Christmas Day. We are having turkey and all the trimmings this year, a first for us. I am listening to "Bing Crosby Christmas" CD as I email all of you. We have a tree this year and actually have a fair amount of presents! We are excited and have come so far in two years. Britt will not be with us this year as she is in Kentucky. We have been missing her greatly and have shed quite a few tears for her. Mostly in thankfulness in the turn around in her life. A few because we miss her smile and sharp sense of humor. She has been in Kentucky for a couple of months now and is already picked up a southern drawl. I know that only from her emails! She is doing so well and we are so proud of her, and I am thankful she didn't rebel as much as her mother did! She has a lot of snow too and has been snowed in for two days. Although she is enjoying the snow so much this year.

We think of Dad less and less as the years go by but this time of year was his favorite. Dad was the spirit of Christmas in our house and made everyone else excited. It took us many years to enjoy Christmas again after he was gone, and it will never be the same without him. It became a tradition for him to do all his shopping on Christmas Eve. A tradition I hated as a teen but loved when I got older. He would get on the phone around 8:00 a.m. with his list in hand. When I lived at home, it would be me on the phone on his behalf! He would call around and find out which stores had exactly what he was looking for, then we would get in the truck and be off. It always amazed me that the rest of us would take a week or a month to shop for Christmas, and he would take 2 hours max. He always bought the best, most unique gifts for everyone. No one could ever guess what he bought for them. He always received socks or some other boring gift in return, and you would think that he got a treasure!

As I got older, I tried to out do him on surprise gifts; but he always surprised me the most. He loved having a house full of people and especially kids. He loved to watch the kids run around and play. The noisier the better, he would crank up the TV and pretend he wasn't paying any attention; but he always was. Then Mom would yell to turn the TV down (I think he always did that on purpose). First there were little Shelly and Kristyn, Travis and Shawn. Then Britt and Trenton. The older he got, the more he loved kids. I can still remember the look on his face. Then there is the memory of him sitting in his lazy boy, towel on his lap, feet crossed at the ankles with a big plate of food in his hands. A big "cold cold cold" glass of milk at his side.

We also were able to make Christmas cookies this year. 3 different kinds which believe it or not is rather amazing. There was nothing better than my Aunt Jan's Christmas cookies. I swear she made 20 different kinds. Of course, when you are a child everything looks bigger and better. I loved going to Aunt Jan's for Christmas. That was my favorite place as a child and even when I was older. To me she was the best Aunt and the coolest lady when I was older. I secretly wanted to be just like her when I grew up. I remember when she started belly dancing...who can say that about their aunt?! Her house was always filled with laughter and adults sitting around chatting at Christmas. Us kids would put on this silly little play every year and I think we must have stayed until after midnight! In my memories, Aunt Jan was this magnetic woman for me. When she was around, there was no one else in the room. She had such a laugh, I can still hear her sometimes if I think hard. I think she was a lady who was independent when it was not "fashionable" for women to be so. I am sure she would have approved of Mom and I being here and she would have been visiting us all the time. Aunt Jan would love it here. (for those of you who are reading this in the book, Laurel's Aunt Jan had MS, was a very courageous woman, my sister, and she passed away at a very young age of a brain aneurysm.)

This Christmas Eve I have been thinking back on families and Christmas' past. I wanted to share some of those memories with all of you. We miss our families at times like these, try to remember Christmas past and take some time to visit with your families this Christmas. Not just your immediate families you see every day but the ones who maybe are long forgotten because we have not forgotten you.

Merry Christmas and God Bless all of you this New Year. May you find what makes you truly happy.

Love from all of us here in warm Cancun!

Laurel, Ruth, Trenton and Fargo!
Armando

A New Man Enters My Life

A lot of things happened to us that spring of 2004. We obtained Palemon, we lost Britt for a while, and my boyfriend moved in with me. I had met Armando in June of 2003 as I was out walking Fargo one evening. He and I, as I said, walked for hours every night. Well, one fateful evening I came upon a security guard standing along the sidewalk. I said hola, and he did also. He asked me about my dog in Spanish, of course, because he could not speak a lick of English; I talked for a little bit and went on my merry way. Well, I had to pass the same way on my way home, and there he was waiting and started talking to me again. He asked if I had a man in my life, and I told him no, that I did not need one. I had no intentions of getting involved with anyone again. No more, nunca! He asked if I was going to be walking that way again the next night, and I told him probably not.

I avoided that way for quite a while, and one day as we were walking, I ran into him again. He was much younger than I, and he asked me to go out with him. I told him no, that I was too old and that he needed to find someone younger, more his own age. He asked me for my cell number, and I gave it to him. I would run into him every now and then, and we would talk a bit, and then I would move on. One evening, as I was out walking Fargo, he called me on my cell. He asked me if I wanted to go to the disco with him. I just laughed and said a great big no and hung up. I was laughing to myself, thinking, *What in the world would I wear to a disco?* As time went on, I did not see him for quite a while. Then one evening, I ran into him again, and I was kind of glad to see him. *Hmm*…right before Christmas of 2003, I ran into him again during the day. He again asked me out. I again told him that I was too old and he needed to find someone more his own age.

He was very persistent, and I finally asked him what he liked to do. We made plans to meet at a certain beach on his day off. Oh boy, what was I getting myself into? I wanted to drive so that if I needed to leave, I would have my truck there, and he would have the bus for transportation. I got there on time and was supposed to meet him out front at a certain restaurant. I sat out there, waiting and waiting, feeling more like a fool as the minutes passed. After about ten minutes of waiting, I decided to call and find out where he was and tell him I was ready to leave. Just as I was starting to dial, he got off the bus. I had never seen him in anything other than a uniform before. We went out to the beach and sat down on towels that I had brought. We sat and talked as much as we could. I had brought my Spanish/English dictionary just in case and did end up using it a few times. My Spanish was getting better and better, and it was not much of a problem at all. We stayed until almost sunset, and then I offered to take him home. It ended up that he only lived about three miles farther out than I did, actually only about five to seven minutes away.

I asked him what he was doing New Year's Eve, and we made plans to go out. So during New Year's Eve, Laurel and Lalo and Armando and I went out. We had such a good time, and I think I got home around 5:00 a.m. the next day! Wow, not bad for an old lady! We started seeing each other quite steadily after that and finally decided it would be much easier if he would just move in because of my working twelve to fourteen hours a day and him working twelve hours, six days a week. Yes, that is the schedule for most workers down there—six twelve-hour days. Yuck! Armando and I lived together until I left Mexico. He was a wonderful singer and played the guitar; he was self-taught. He could also play the marimbas and an accordion. In the many evenings in our two years together, we would go to the Caribbean, take the dogs, and the guitar, and he would play and sing to me. It was very romantic, and I loved every minute of it. Who wouldn't? Right?

Pablo's Wedding

I n the Spring of 2004, we also had a wedding "in the family." I say this because our guys felt to us like family. Pablo informed us that he and Adrianna were getting married. We were very excited for him as he was. He and Adrianna had been dating for several years. When you get married in Mexico, you first get married by the government. Then if you want a church marriage, that comes after. Pablo and Adrianna had found a house that they wanted to buy. One of the taxes that we as employers were paying is a tax that goes toward a fund that the employees can apply for which helps them buy a house. They get points added up for every year that they are employed and when they have so many points, they then can use them toward a purchase of a house. We had to fill out papers for Pablo so that he could qualify for these points and also qualify for a loan to buy the house. They purchased the house before they were married but did not move into the house until they were actually married. He had been living at home with his parents whom we had met several times. She also lived with her mother, whom we had also met.

They did not actually move in together until after their marriage in the church. Even though they were legally married by the government, they did not consider it to be a marriage until they were married by the priest. We thought that was cool. Once again, we thought what a fine upstanding Christian we have working for us. Laurel and I were invited to the wedding. Also, at this time, I would like to introduce Carol and Bob and Cheryl and Garnet into this story. These are two couples that we met in April of 2003 as tourists that went out on our boat. They were in a group of people of tourists, but they stood out to us and soon became very dear friends. They came out on our boat two or three times that time when they were down and again in November. When they would come down, they always brought us gifts, wonderful Christian books, and something for our guys and Palemon's children as well.

When they would come down, we always knew that we were going to have two good weeks because Carol would talk to everyone telling them about our tour and how wonderful it was. We will always be very grateful for their friendship and help. They were so close to our guys on the boat from going out so many times that Pablo asked them to come to the wedding as well. Carol and Bob did go. The wedding was very beautiful; Adrianna was so pretty, and Pablo was so handsome. We were very proud of both of them and had a wonderful time at the reception. Of course, we were the only white gringas there, but it did not matter. We were always treated with much respect, and we thought love from his family.

Carol was so funny; she was up in the church during the ceremony taking pictures. She is known for all the pictures she takes. She had a blast during the ceremony and also at the reception. So our Pablo was finally a married man, and they moved into their house. He had a week's vacation coming, and we added more days for an added wedding gift. Before they had moved into their house, they had purchased a refrigerator, some other appliances, and some furniture. Well, the house was sitting empty with all that stuff in it, so of course, it got broken into, and they stole everything that they had bought. It is so sad, but that is why people live behind bars and walls and have security guards everywhere. Of course, they were not insured as we would be here in the United States. You suck it up and start again. It was a very nice house and a nice neighborhood. They had taken us out to see the house when they got it. They were so proud and happy, and we were happy for them too.

Time to Move the Boat Once Again

After Palemon had been working for us for a while, we were getting more and more unhappy with the restaurant where we had had the boat, Las Jaibas. The owner was rarely there, and the place was being ran by his young son. The waitresses that worked (and I use that word lightly) were lazier than a pack of pet raccoons. They never cleaned the place before they left in the evening, and they were never that busy! The bathroom was always dirty; they never had toilet paper in the restroom nor soap to wash your hands. Laurel and I had to make sure that we were there in plenty of time to clean up the restaurant area, the bar area, and the bathroom. We had to bring our own toilet paper and hand soap and try to remember to take it when we left; otherwise, their customers would use it during the day. We were getting more and more unhappy with the place. We also had been presented a bill of $2,000 pesos being similar to $200.00 U.S. dollars for the owner to go and get our boat that day when the wind took it up to Punta Sam.

At that time, we were also informed that approximately two weeks after our boat had been painted, there had been a fire at the Hacienda del Mar, and black smoke had blown over to our boat. An insurance representative had come over to see if there had been any damage done to our boat. Well, our captain at that time, Cesar, told the insurance rep that yes, the smoke damaged the paint. That he would put the claim in for it and that the owners of the boat did not need to be notified! We knew nothing about this up until this time. No one said anything to us, not the owner of the restaurant and not our "good friend" Pablo. As it turned out, we contacted the insurance company before they had sent out any checks. We told them what our previous captain had done, and they changed the name on the claim to Two Much Fun-N-A Boat. We did get the damage check. It just about paid for the demanda that Cesar had put on us but definitely not for the attorney fees. We also paid for the tow.

Palemon knew we were unhappy at Las Jaibas and suggested moving the boat down to Blue Bay. We did not think in our wildest dreams that Blue Bay would let us dock our boat there, but it never hurts to ask, right? Laurel and I went down there one day after the boat went out on a tour. We found our way into the marina manager, and he turned out to be a really nice guy. He told us that he did have room for our boat and gave us a price (which was comparable to what we had been paying in Puerta Juarez plus paying for a van service). If we could eliminate the van service, we might actually be able to get a salary! We became very excited over that! It was really weird for us to think that our boat may be docked at Blue Bay because Blue Bay was where we went on our first tour back in 1996 as fresh tourists. There were a few problems however of putting our boat there. Of course there was!

The water at the dock where he had a spot to put our boat was not very deep. Our boat only drew three feet of water, but it did need the three feet and then some when we left the dock with twenty-five people on board. We went back to our boat to greet the people that afternoon, and then we talked with Palemon. Palemon and Pablo went with us over to Blue Bay and checked things out. Palemon and Armando, the marina manager, both suggested that we would be able to suck the sand out of where we needed to put our boat and send it elsewhere. So that is what we did. At the end of the month when our rent was due once again at Las Jaibas, we moved our boat to Blue Bay. Well, there were two other much larger tri-marans going out of Blue Bay at that time, so we were not greeted (once again) with open arms. There were many comments by the other boat workers on how they wished their bosses would look like us, and our guys took a razzing all the time for working for two American women. They were very used to this by now and so were we, just another day at work in Mexico.

Eventually, our guys got enough sand sucked out so we could get the boat in where it belonged. Laurel and I both helped and my boyfriend, Armando, was also there helping. Palemon brought his wife and kids and new baby girl and put up our shade canvas that we had. The kids had a ball swimming and were playing around. His little girl, Dona, never did take to Laurel and me. Every time she was near us, she would start crying. I do not think that we ever got to hold her the entire time that Palemon worked for us. We just loved his wife; she was such a sweet thing. She did not, however, speak any English nor did his children. Palemon was very fluent in English, all self-taught, but he had never tried to teach his children. They had no interest in learning even though that is how you are able to get some of the decent employment down there. We tried to encourage Palemon to teach his children, but when you work six days a week, it is kind of hard I guess.

Shortly after the boat arrived in Cancun and as soon as we started running tours, we had to get a new motor. Our motor was too small, only a fifteen horsepower, and it did not work good. While we were docked at Las Jaibas, the owner had told us about a motor that he knew of for sale. Of course, it was a used motor. There was no way we could have afforded a new motor. This one would break down with disgusting regularity, and our old captain knew a boat mechanic…go figure. So we always had a place to take our motor when it needed fixing like the time we were all out on the boat before we were up and running with tours and the motor fell off in the middle of the Caribbean! Yeah, it did! One of Laurel's friends at the time, Juan, who was a certified dive master, dove into the water and got a hold of it. He tied a rope on it, and Cesar, Pablo and I hauled the thing out of the water and back onto the boat. We had to go immediately to shore. Cesar then tore the motor apart, sprayed it with fresh water, and sprayed every part with WD 40. We then took it right over to the mechanic. I just remembered that little adventure in our lives down there. It is hard to remember all the things that happened to us. . However, in August of 2004, I finally started to try and keep a journal.

Mexican Jail

I returned back to Mexico from a two-week vacation in Michigan. My girlfriends and I took the horses to the Upper Peninsula of Michigan. It took me forty-seven years, but I finally made it! On August 12, 2004, after the boat left, Laurel and I had some running around to do for the business. We went to the bank, etcetera. At about 10:30 a.m., we were returning home. Thank God we had to take my truck that day to get gas for the boat! I was waiting at the intersection of Bonampak and Colasial heading west. Colasial is the highway that you take out to the airport for those of you who have been to Cancun before. I was first in line, waiting at the light. When it turned green, I went, and a dump truck loaded with sand seemed to appear from nowhere. He was on my left. I said, "Oh my God, there is a big truck!" and we then got smashed! He caught the very back of my door, my whole side back to my rear tire. He spun my truck 190 degrees. I had my seat belt on, Laurel did not. The dump truck continued on past and slammed into the light pole. That is what stopped him. Then the horror began.

Laurel and I sat there, looking at each other. The next thing we knew I had a microphone stuck in my face and someone asking us how I felt! Well, I was crying at the time, so he should have had a clue! Laurel finally piped up and told him exactly how we felt! She said, "The son of a —— ran a red light and smashed into us. How do you think we feel?" Of course, when it was aired on TV, they did not use those words! Oh yes, TV no less, plus we were in the paper! We sat in the truck, and some of the police in black, who were by the way parked very near the accident and had to have seen the whole thing, came over to the truck. One was talking to us very nicely and said he saw it, and that the guy did run the red light. By this time, there were police all over the place. Laurel got out of the truck at some point and started trying to defend us because as time went on, everything was our fault. It was very obvious when the driver of the truck was out walking around; he was very, very drunk. He was strutting around the place like a proud hunter who had just killed the biggest dear or bear in the woods! It took them about two hours to get their act together and tow the dump truck away and have me move my truck out of the intersection. Then I did not comprehend where they wanted me to move it. Of course, I was in shock and had been crying the whole entire time. I finally got it moved and out of the way sitting on the left side of the road right next to all the oncoming traffic where everyone going by could see my truck and me sitting there crying like a baby! When it came time to move my truck, a policeman got in the truck with me. No explanations at all. He rode with me to take my truck to be impounded.

I need to back up. Right after the accident happened, Laurel called Lalo to come, and he did. So he was there and able to tell us a little of what was going on, as always!

When we got to the impound place, everyone was so rude, and we were again treated like criminals. We needed to unload several cases of empty *kawamas* (those are very large beer bottles) and boxes from the back of my truck. I always had empty boxes of beer bottles in the back of my truck because when we would buy beer for the boat, we would buy several cases at a time and turn in the empties. We pulled into this fenced area as instructed, and Lalo pulled in behind us so that he could put the stuff in his car. The police had a fit that he was in there, and he had to back out immediately. I had to be out of the fenced area before we could unload anything from my truck. The tránsito (that is traffic police) were not going to let me back out, and Laurel was arguing with them. I practically had to run them over before they would let me out of the fenced area once again. Lalo was forced to park down the road quite a way from us, and he and Laurel carried everything from the truck to the car. Then I had to pull into the fenced area again. All of the time that Lalo was moving stuff, these illiterate jerks were yelling at me and mumbling to do this and that. We kept saying, "No intiendo," and one guy in particular would answer, "Uh?"

After I pulled in, I think the only decent person there, another transito, had to make an inventory list of what was on and in the truck. He proceeded to do his job, and he did speak a little English. I had, by then, called Armando, and he was trying to find me. He started from the Crucero and went to the judicial building where I was going to be taken. He waited there awhile and got in a taxi and headed out to Bonfil. After many phone calls and frustrating conversations, he managed to find me. Then they would not let him in to where I was. Then someone would say he could come in; he would start in, and someone else would yell at him for being in there, so he would turn around and walk out. This happened several times before they finally let him in. After the inventory, all in Spanish of course, I had to go through the list before I signed it. Laurel and I finally agreed that it was okay to sign. Then I drove my poor truck down to its parking place. I had to crawl over to the passenger seat because my door would not open. I had my first look at my poor truck. I started crying all over again! I was carrying my hitch receiver, papers, and other things that I wanted to remove from my truck. My cap on the truck was split right apart in the back and was totally trashed. After walking up to the front, I then was taken in a police car down to the police station on Coba. Armando was able to ride with me in the patrol car. I did not know that I was under arrest. Laurel had contacted Kevin right off the bat for an attorney. Kevin called a few attorneys and got a hold of Veronica, an attorney that we had used for employee contracts for the company. She called a friend of hers, and he met us at the police station.

After about an hour of sitting in a room watching amazing incompetence at work and a report being typed on a typewriter that had to be around seventy-five years old, I was taken into a room for a reading/eyesight exam. I had no problem reading the whole chart for them with my distance eye, but they then tried to make me read it with my close-up eye, which I could not do. I wear mono vision contacts. I then had to explain in Spanish that I had contacts and one eye is used for reading and one for distance. Of course, I do not think they had ever heard of such a thing. Then they asked if I had been drinking alcohol. I just looked at them and said, disgustedly, *no*. After that, I was taken back to the room and just sat there, not knowing anything that was going on. Armando was in the room with me, and Laurel and Lalo were out in the hallway somewhere. I could hear arguing going on, and I could also understand that the owner of the dump truck was there arguing and tried to talk Laurel into not hiring an attorney. At that point, I had taken off all my valuable jewelry and given it to Armando to take home.

The attorney, Laurel, Lalo, and the police came for me, and we all walked together down this hallway. We stopped at a desk in the middle of a hallway. I was told to give Laurel my cell phone. Lalo had disappeared. Laurel was standing there saying, "No, don't go," and I was led away to jail. I had to give them all my jewelry. There were a couple of rings that I could not get off my fingers and one I could but pretended that I couldn't. Right in front of me was the guy that had hit me. They had just taken his hat; that is all he had and told him to go sit down. The next thing was that I was instructed to do the same. We were put into a room with four chairs on each side of the room (a little room), and there was a policeman sitting at the entrance of this room, answering the phone, taking emergency calls. He had a gun and always had his back to us. I could have pulled the gun out and shot him if I was so inclined to do so. There we sat all day and well into the night with the drunk that hit me! His eyes were all red, and he kept sniffing snot into his mouth and spitting it out the window. Either that or he would blow his nose into the bottom of his shirt. It was disgusting to say the least! He slept off and on the entire time, but not me. I sat and sobbed.

The cop that checked me in spoke a little English and, at one point, tried to carry on a conversation. I could not talk; I just started crying. At some point in time later in the day, my family and friends had food and a big bottle of water delivered to me. I could not eat at that time, but I did drink the water. Later, this woman came in and asked me a few questions. She then did a sort of drunk test on the guy. She went away. A police officer delivered a note to me from Laurel saying that a doctor was going to check me and Laurel said to pretend to be hurting really bad. By that time, I pretty much was. She came in to get me just after I got the note, so I had to walk and read at the same time. I did not know that she was the doctor. She had me take my shirt off, kind of checked me, and sent me back.

I then sat and did a lot of talking to God. I did try to eat something because, by then, I figured I would be there for the night. When the doctor had brought me out to that room, there stood all my family and friends. I started crying once again, and Laurel came over and gave me a great, big hug! She said I looked like death. When I came out of the room, the cop that had tried to talk to me earlier escorted me back. I stopped to talk to Laurel briefly and told her that she was *not* to pay anybody any money to get me out, that I would spend the night. I did this in front of the guy that spoke a little English, hoping that if they had bribery in mind to forget it!

When I tried to eat, it was very difficult to chew and swallow, but I did. I did not know if they would take the stuff from me or not. On toward evening, I figured Laurel and my friends had left. Then I got a very nice surprise my family sent me in a Coke. I knew the attorney, Laurel, Elvia, Raul, and Hannah were there fighting to get me released to Raul (he was my doctor and brother-in-law to Kevin) and the hospital. Around 9:00 p.m., they took the guy and put him in a cell. Then an older guy (police) came up to me and told me if I wanted to lie down to rest, I could go in a cell, and they would leave the door open. I told him that I thought that I was going to be taken to the hospital. He asked the guard, and the guard said, "Yes, that was true." Well, about one and a half hours later, two plainclothes cops said to me that they were taking me to a doctor. I started taking my stuff (food and water), and they told me that I could leave it and that I would be back.

At that point after them telling me that I would be back, I did not know where I was going. They took me outside to a Volkswagen and pointed to the backseat. I told them I could not get in. It did not matter; I had to anyway. Therefore, one cop rode with my knees in his back the entire trip. When we pulled out, there was everybody! Laurel, Lalo, Armando, Elvia, Trenton, Hannah, boy what a welcome sight! They told me I was going to see Raul. Then I knew I would not be spending the night in jail. The attorney rode in the car with me. He was talking to the cops the entire time. They did not think I would understand, but I heard them ask the attorney about how much money I had. He told them that I did not have any.

When I walked into the clinic, Raul was standing right there, waiting for me! What a welcome and blessed site! He checked me over, fit me with a neck brace, had X-rays taken, and admitted me. He started an IV right away, pain shot, and other medications. I saw Trenton and Armando and sent them on their way. Armando had been up for more than twenty-four hours by then. Trenton spent the night at the house with Armando. They were back at the hospital at 9:00 a.m. the next morning. Armando left around noon to get a few hours of sleep before work. Trenton spent the day with me. Laurel came about 4:00 or 5:00 p.m. after the tour. She showed up again around 8:00 p.m. or 9:00 p.m. and said, "You are free!" The police had a guard posted all the time that I was in the hospital so I would not escape.

Once again, after leaving the hospital, I had to go down to the station and sign some papers. Hannah, Kevin's wife, read everything for me to make sure what I was signing was okay. I then went home. What a great feeling! I called Armando and let him know that I was home. He was very happy. I was very weak and very pale for quite a few days. I stayed in bed and did nothing but lie there, thankful to God that I was okay, Laurel was okay, and I was no longer in jail and at home in my own bed. What an ordeal! I pray that I never have to go through anything like that again.

A few days after I was released, we met with the attorney. During the whole process, Laurel had asked him three or four times what his rates were going to be. He kept telling her not to worry about it. Hannah had gone with us to interpret, and he informed us that the amount owed to him so far was US $2,500! Oh my God! Then he told us that he projected that the case would be dragged out costing another US $2,500 to boot! I am an American; I could afford it, right? Elvia is Hannah's sister, Kevin's sister-in-law, and had done our accounting for us when we first got started and refused to be paid. When Elvia found out about how much this attorney was going to charge us, she had a fit. She talked to her friend whose husband is an attorney, and he said that was way out of line to charge. We met with him a couple of days later and paid him $2,000 pesos similar to $200.00 U.S dollars to go and check out the case.

The next afternoon, I got a phone call from Laurel stating that she had just spoken with Elvia, and Elvia had told her that the new attorney had just found out that the other attorney had lied and that I was found guilty! I started crying again. I could see myself in jail until I paid for the lousy dump truck to be fixed not to mention paying for my truck! Laurel called me back a little later and said, "Get ready. Lalo and I are picking you up in about ten minutes." I figured that they were taking me down to the police station again. *No*, we were going to meet the attorney. He told us that I had missed two hearings. He also needed me to go into court with my FM3 so that he could look over the case.

There was a hearing for the family of the guy to pay for my truck. It turned out that the first attorney had approved the price of 11,000 pesos (around $1,100.00 US. Dollars) pesos to repair my truck. What a joke. I told my attorney it would take at least 50,000 pesos (around $5,000.00 U.S. dollars) to repair it. My attorney then informed the drunk's girlfriend that it was going to take 50,000 pesos to repair my truck. She told him that they do not have that kind of money and that he would have to be in jail until they could pay me. We then went to El Cafe on Nader to talk things over. We decided to go after the woman that owns the company that he worked for. It turned out that she fired the driver when he was found guilty. This released her from any responsibility, and she was able to get her dump truck out of the impound. My attorney also found out that the judge was on vacation and that I would not be able to get my truck out until he got back, which was September 6. We had to put a demand on the owner of the company.

I am going to finish the story about the truck in this chapter, but I do not want to make it sound like it was a slam-bang-thank-you kind of thing that was over in a short period. Not in Mexico, it isn't! The first court date came, and Laurel and Lalo had to go in and testify. In Mexico when something like this happens, you have to have three witnesses. It does not matter if only one person was there and saw what happened. You *have* to produce three witnesses! Lalo became my third witness. I was number 1, Laurel was number 2, and Lalo was number 3. That is why Laurel and Lalo had to testify. Then came my first turn. It was nothing like you would think. You go to where the judge is. There are also prisoners being held in this building and a lot of commotion going on everywhere. Someone sits at a computer, types in all the information that I had already given three times previous to this day, my attorney looks over the statement, tells me it is okay to sign, and then I signed. Then the guy that hit me got to do the same.

Every time this man made a statement, the story changed. He also had a transitó (that is a traffic cop) testify on his behalf. *Nice!* At least the guy showed up for this; he had no choice as he was in jail at that time. This whole deal was supposed to take place two more times. You have three chances to prove yourself innocent. The next time that I had to go, the place had been changed out to the prison. You have to walk through wired gates, sign you name, and show your ID. I had to show my FM3. The first time I went out there, I was taken there by the police.

One morning as I was getting ready for the tour, I had a knock at my door. There were two police officers at my door, and they are going to take me away because I had missed my court date. I missed it because I was never notified. I went next door and got my neighbor who spoke very good English. I had him read the paper that they had for me and tell me what the heck was going on. I had no money on my cell phone and could not call Laurel to let her know what was going on. I asked my neighbor to let Laurel know when she came to get me what had happened to me! The police were very nice to me, and one of them even gave me his phone card to use at a pay phone that they stopped at so that I could call my attorney. Now those guys were an exception, believe me!

My attorney met me at the prison, and we proceeded from there. I gave my testimony with an interpreter there. The guy was okay but not really fluent in English and not too bright I guess would be a nice way of stating this. Anyway, I got through another ordeal, and Laurel met me out there and gave me a ride home. On the next notification that I received, Armando went out there with me. It is a good thing that he did because my attorney never showed up, and we were finally informed that the hearing was cancelled until a later date. When the next hearing came, I went and my attorney was there, but the guy that hit me never showed up. By this time, they had let him out of prison. After that, Laurel and I kept stopping at my attorney's office, and he was never there. By this time, I had paid him US $1,200 for his services.

His services also included getting my truck out of impound. On September 14 I had an appointment with the attorney and the judge to get my truck back. After Laurel, Trenton, and I waited at the judge's office for an hour for my attorney to show up, the judge decided that he wanted my truck title translated into Spanish. The judge also had a problem with my name on the title because on the title it was Ruth Gonyaw and on my FM3 it is Ruth Laurel Gonyaw. I had to pay $400 pesos (around $40.00 U.S.) to have my title translated, and the guy did it incorrectly. So it was another wasted trip out to the judge. I figured he wanted bribe money.

On September 15, I had another appointment with the judge at 9:00 a.m. Laurel and I went there (Laurel was also leaving that day for the United States), and my attorney did not show up until 9:45 a.m. Nothing had been done about my truck title, so I had to leave and wait for a call from my attorney. In the meantime, I had to get Laurel and Lalo to the airport as they were supposed to be there by 11:00 a.m. to leave for the United States. I finally got a call from my attorney at 4:30 p.m. I went straight to the judge's office, and my attorney showed up there shortly after. Then we waited. The judge finally signed the paper releasing my truck, and we got out of there at 5:30 p.m. I ended up having to pay the judge $300 pesos (around $30.00 U.S.) for working late. By this time, it was too late to go out to get my truck. This again I am going to take straight from my journal.

September 17, 2004

Armando and I met my attorney at 9:30 a.m. We went out to get my truck at the impound in Bonfil. Well, of course, it was not as easy as my attorney perceived it would be. We had to go back to the transitó. I had to go into the commandant's office. He sits in this chair and reminded me of a king who sits on his throne, and everyone kowtows to him. He had to have weighed close to four hundred pounds. The big deal going down at the time was filling out forms for new pants and shirts. I had to sit there while all this was discussed. Then I watched a game of payoff while I was sitting there. The transitós came out of the woodwork like cockroaches and crowded into another office. Everybody has to get a piece of the pie. He finally looked over the paperwork and gave my attorney a piece of paper to go pay.

We went to a window and paid, but that is not the end of it. They of course had to have copies of my FM3, truck title, registration, and the judge's ruling. By this time, it was 11:30, and my attorney had to go to another appointment. His secretary finished up for me at another building. We had to walk over to another building next door. They had to actually see me with my FM3. Then they stamped something, and then we could finally go get my truck. When we got there, I had to wait while a guy and the secretary walked in to get my truck. I was not allowed to go into the fenced area. After waiting another ten minutes or so, they finally brought my truck out, and it was finally mine once again! It was in the compound for six weeks! It was very ironic, I thought at that time, and now, the title that was okay to get my truck into Mexico suddenly had to be translated so that I could get my truck out of car jail! After I got my truck, one would think, as all my friends and family were thinking at that time, that it was time to pack that baby up and get the heck out of Mexico! Didn't I tell you we were stubborn?

I had to get an estimate to have my truck repaired. Actually, my attorney kept telling me that I needed to have it repaired and then sue for the money. Well, I got an estimate at the Chevrolet dealer after some difficulty that I will not go into detail about, and the estimate was US $5,000. I did not have that kind of money to repair my truck, so I gave the estimate to my attorney. As I stated earlier, after I got my truck, Laurel and I would go to the attorney's office to try to talk to him and see what else was going on with my case. He was never in and never would return any phone calls. After months of waiting to get my truck fixed, Laurel and I one morning after the boat went out went to his office and waited for him. We waited and waited until he finally showed up. He had to talk to us now. At this point in time, all I wanted from him was a copy of my court papers and a receipt for the $1,200 that I had paid him in cash and never gotten a receipt. He told me to come back and that he could not get that ready while we waited. He had to "find" my file.

When we returned, we returned with Brittnay. Brittnay is very fluent in Spanish and pretty much told him what we were all thinking of him at the time for his great "service." He actually told Laurel and Brittnay to leave his office and for me to return for the papers later. We did not leave but waited out in his driveway so that he could not leave. When he finally got the things ready that I had been asking for, he called me back into his office, would not let Laurel nor Brittnay in, and gave me my things. Needless to say, my truck never was repaired, and I eventually drove it back home to Michigan all smashed up.

The Sunday Meetings

About a year into working with Thomas Moore and the Royal Resorts, one of the Thomas Moore reps asked Laurel and I on one of our visits why we did not come to the welcoming parties on Sundays? We looked at him and at each other and said, "Because we didn't know that we could!" Miguel is the one that asked us and told us to come in on Sunday and have some fliers to pass out, and he would get us to the party! So we did, and that is when things really started happening for us as far as getting more people out on the boat. You see, the Royal Resorts are time-share resorts, and every Sunday morning, they have a welcoming meeting in the morning where they explain many different things about Cancun to their new arrivals. Then around noon, they have a welcoming party with free drinks, music, dancing, and little contests and give out prizes and also serve lunch. Miguel took us out there and introduced us to the head honcho and told him that we were going to be out there handing out fliers for our tour.

It was a very difficult thing for Laurel and me to do. We would walk around and introduce ourselves to people, hand them a flier, and try to explain our tour a little. It was difficult because we felt like we were bothering people when they were trying to have a good time. We stayed together for the first few Sundays, and then we felt we could cover more people if we would separate. This is how we kind of got our foot in the door, you might say, with the whole Sunday meeting thing. After a couple of months of doing this, we got invited to the meetings. We would pass out our fliers to everyone coming into the meetings. At that time, there was another boat company working with Thomas Moore, and their boat was moored out in front of the VCI, which is one of the Royal Resorts. The captain of this tour boat would also come to the meetings and give us the glare because we were now invading his territory.

This particular boat had been working with the Royals for close to twenty years by this time and were kind of an old shoe around the place. We were the fresh, new pair of shoes and were not liked or appreciated much by the old shoe. Half of the time, the captain who had been passing out the fliers did not show at the meetings and pretty soon stopped coming altogether. After a few months of going to the meetings and passing out our fliers and talking to people, greeting old customers who were returning, and getting to feel at home at the Royals, we were suddenly allowed to speak at the meeting and tell people about our tour. Breakthrough after breakthrough! There were five Royal Resorts at that time; three of them were very close together, and you could run from one to the other for both meetings. Then there was the Royal Sands, which was apart from the three, and the VCI, which was separate also. One of us would go to the Royal Sands for both meetings, and one of us would go to the three connected and go to all six meetings. I took the Sands; Laurel got the big job! Age does have it's privileges sometimes. The fact that we were able to go to these meetings by the grace of God kept us alive and let us hang in there for as long as we did. We loved the personal contact with the people, and most of the people were very receptive to us. This was the beginning of our success if you want to call it that.

Time to Move the Boat Once Again

Shortly after the accident, we were notified by Blue Bay that we were going to have to move our boat. It could no longer be moored at their dock as they were planning on expanding and getting Sea Do's to rent and wanted the dock space all for Blue Bay activities. *Great, where are we going to go now?* we were wondering. There are not that many places to rent dock space in the hotel zone, and we were running out of places. We went up the beach toward town. We knew of the dock at Las Perlas, so we decided to go there and check things out after our boat went out on a tour. We needed to find a place before everyone else got a space somewhere else and we were left hanging. We pulled into Las Perlas and immediately ran into one of the dive boat owners, whom we knew slightly from running into him in the harbor master's office and such. We asked him if he knew if there was any dock space available for rent here at Las Perlas. This is where he had his boat docked, so we knew he would know if there were any spaces available. He told us, "No, there is no space for a sailboat."

We said, "Oh, okay, thanks," and got back in the car. We looked at each other and decided that we were not going to take his word for it. So we got back out of the car and went into the hotel to find out who we could talk to about dock space. We were directed to the correct person, and it just so happened that he was there. He was the marina manager, was French, and spoke French, Spanish, and a little English. So between his bad English and our bad Spanish, we found out that there was indeed space for our boat there; the water was very deep, and it would be a great place for our boat. The only problem with this place was that the marina was separate from the hotel; therefore, our people would not be able to go through the hotel to get to the boat. There was a public beach right next door, so that was how we had to get our people to our boat. They would arrive at Las Perlas; we would meet them out on the sidewalk and walk them down to the public beach and then back down the beach to our boat. Once we got them to the dock, if they needed to use the restroom, we were allowed to take them from the beach area up to the bathroom where they could use the facilities. We had to decide where we were going to serve our continental breakfast. We decided that we would serve it at the public beach under some of the palm trees.

Every time that we moved our boat, we had to make a new map and a description of our tour, where it was leaving from, where it was going, the times and draw a map.

When we decided to move our boat from Las Jaibas, it was suggested to us by some of the reps at Thomas Moore to ask the Royal Resorts permission to dock our boat at the VCI dock. We were told what office we needed to go in and who we needed to talk to, so in we went. We told the secretary who we were and asked to speak to señor so and so (I no longer remember his name.). He was in the office and did see us, and we told him what we wanted. He said that that would have to be taken up with the board of directors in their next meeting. He told us to type up a proposal and give it to him so that he would have something to take to the next meeting. Laurel and I sat down and made up a proposal, saying what we would pay monthly for dockage, what our tours consisted of, and when the boat would be leaving and arriving at the dock. We turned it in immediately, and then we kept stopping into his office to ask if he had heard anything from the board. This went on for a couple of months with still no answer.

We then took it upon ourselves to stop and talk to the attorney that handles everything for the Royals. We just walked into the office after finding out where it was with no appointment or notification. We told his secretary what it was that we wanted, and she went in his office to let him know that we were there and what we wanted. He saw us right away, and we told him that we had asked permission to dock our boat at the VCI and had been waiting and waiting for an answer with no luck. He told us he would see what he could do for us; we gave him our cell phone numbers and left. A few weeks later, about the time that we were moving our boat over to Las Perlas, he called me. He told me that the board had decided that they did not want another boat docked at the VCI. I told him thank you very much and that I had another question. I asked him if we could get permission to go over to the VCI to pick up the people from the Royal Resorts. He said he did not see why we would not be able to do that, but he would need to check and would get right back with me. A few days later, that is exactly what he did. He told me that we did get permission to pick up all the Royal Resort people right there at the VCI dock. What a blessing that was for us. Once again, God was good to us.

We had to go and meet with the head of security and explain exactly what we would be doing daily and were told where to enter the hotel and where to walk around through the hotel and around the pool area out to the beach and to the dock. We were also instructed as to where our men would be able to walk through with supplies for the boat. Then we started our new routine of leaving Las Perlas and motoring over to the VCI dock to pick up the people. Laurel and I decided that it would be great to serve the continental breakfast out at the end of the dock. It was perfect; it is very large and shaped in a T with a little palapa built on one end of the T and a stainless steel table built on the other end of the T with some benches for people to sit down if they wished. It was a perfect setup for us, and we made ourselves right at home.

It was wonderful walking out there early in the morning and greeting some of the people staying at the VCI. A lot of them would talk to us every morning after the boat left or in the evening after our boat was returning to Las Perlas after dropping off the people. The Royal Resorts has busses that run from resort to resort, and if you are a member, you are able to use the facilities at each resort if you wish. We changed our tour schedule to accommodate their bus schedule, and we were set! When we would have people come on the tour from our website bookings or from another travel agency, we would greet them at Las Perlas, load them onto the boat, motor over to the VCI, and serve them the continental breakfast as well from the VCI. Once people started seeing our boat there every day, our business started to pick up also.

Ruth carrying supplies out to the boat on the dock of
the Club International of Cancun for a tour.

On Sundays during the welcoming party, Laurel and I started stopping at the VCI, and we would also have our guys dock the boat at the end of the dock with the sails up so people would notice. Pretty soon we were being allowed to speak into the microphone at the parties, letting people know about our tour. We would also spend the time handing out our brochures. That really helped business also. As time went on, the other boat company that had been mooring their boat out front of the VCI were not getting any business from Thomas Moore. They had killed their good reputation with Thomas Moore, and we were getting all the business for anyone that wanted to go sailing and snorkeling. This never did go over very well with the old captain of the boat, and he tried many, many things to get us into trouble with Thomas Moore and the Royal Resorts. He lied about us about certain things several times, and we would get called in for it and have to prove that it was not true. It was a constant struggle almost daily with one thing or another. If it wasn't the boat people, it was the security guards.

Hurricane Season 2004

On September 8, 2004, I had written that we had been getting rain off and on all that day. Florida had been hit by two hurricanes already, Charley and Frances, and now we had gotten the report that number three was possibly on its way. This one was named Ivan. First, it was thought that it was going to go to Florida, but it turned and was supposed to hit Cuba and then the Yukatan (which was us)! It was a category 4 at the time that I was getting this report and writing in my journal. Brittnay was staying with my niece Cathy at the time of the first two hurricanes, the second one being right where they were living. Cathy packed up her and Britt, and they headed for Georgia for a few days and rode Frances out. It was the biggest Florida evacuation ever. On September 9, the report was that Ivan had caused twenty-one deaths already and kept switching back and forth from a 4 to a 5 and back to 4. The path in the newspaper showed Florida again but can switch to the Yukatan. Laurel was packing because she was supposed to leave in six days for Michigan and then Florida to sign Brittnay into the Job Corps.

On Sunday, September 12, 2004, Laurel picked me up to head to the Royals for the Sunday meetings. Ivan was still a category 5 and had killed twenty-one people in Jamaica. It had slowed down and was very big and was supposed to hit west of Cuba and then perhaps the Yukatan or go up and hit west Florida and Louisiana. The waves rolling in at the Royal Sands were huge that day! Laurel and I called Palemon and Pablo and told them we wanted them to move the boat over to Isla Mujeres that afternoon. After talking with people in the Sands, I was very glad that we had called the guys; it had been Laurel's idea, and we ended up sending them earlier than first planned. When the meetings were done, Laurel and I went and got gas cans from the boat and went and bought hurricane supplies for the boat and the guys. The water was only about eight inches from the top of the dock. We could look out across at Isla Mujeres and see the waves rolling across. They looked like boats moving in a row. We had never seen that before and it was very scary!

We sent the guys and boat on their way; we bid them farewell and good luck and prayed. Palemon was so excited to be able to take the boat out into that with the waves rolling so high. He said to me before they left, "This is going to be fun, Jefa, are you sure you don't want to come with us?"

I just looked at him and said, "No thanks, not this time." After supper that night, it started raining cats and dogs. Laurel, Lalo, Armando, and I went shopping for hurricane supplies for our houses. What a treat that was! We had never seen anything like this before in our entire lives! The total population of Cancun was out shopping, it seemed. We first tried the Gigante, which is a grocery store pretty close to my house and the one that I normally shopped at. After fifteen or twenty minutes of trying to get a parking spot in the pouring down rain, we finally got in the door. They had no bread and no water, and lines at the cash registers were the entire length of the store. We left there and went to Walmart out toward Merida way. The whole parking lot was full. We got in the store and there were no carts.

All of the TVs were on and telling us we were probably going to take a direct hit! Laurel and I started grabbing stuff. We each grabbed a box and used that for a cart. Then we spotted big wash pans and used them. People were using garbage containers and anything they could use to put things into. The lines were at least half the store length long. There was no bread or water. Laurel and I did not have a clue what to buy for food, so we just took cans of tuna, beans, cereal, things like that. Armando was with me in line, and Laurel and Lalo were somewhere else in line. We got through around 10:00 p.m., and Lalo did not get through his line until 11:00 p.m.

I was scared, especially for Palemon and Pablo. I called them up on Palemon's cell phone and told them that Isla Mujeres was beginning to be evacuated. I told them that we wanted them to leave the boat and come back to Cancun. Palemon said everything was calm there and that they were staying. We went to bed around midnight. The next morning, Monday, September 13, 2004, I was supposed to go and get my truck. Laurel and Trenton came and picked me up, and that is when I had to have my title translated. This is what I said in my journal at the time,

> The biggest hurricane ever is coming, and my truck is sitting where it will be flooded out! It is now 4:30 p.m., and I still do not have my truck. If we take a direct hit, we will all be gone anyway, and I won't need my truck.

Armando had taped the windows of the house that day; I didn't have a clue. They have evacuated Puerto Juarez; Laurel had called and told me that the hotel zone was closed down and that they feel the tourists will be safer in the hotels than downtown where we were! We were waiting for an important notice at 6:00 p.m. as to whether the eye, which was fifty-five kilometers wide, was going to head toward Cuba or Cancun. Well, thank God so very much, it switched directions and went over more toward Cuba! What a relief that was for us in Cancun. Armando went off to work, and I went to bed! The next day, the sky was blue, and the sun was shining; however, the port was still closed, and there was no work for us. I was still dealing with my truck, trying to get it back and Laurel was thankful she could leave on her vacation the next day.

September 15: Independence Day

The neighbors all had a fiesta together because at midnight, they celebrate their Independence Day. They close off the street and set up tables and chairs in the street, and every family brings a dish to pass. They play music and eat and talk and have a wonderful time. This is how my neighbors celebrated most holidays, and I was always invited. They usually had a piñata for the children, and it is so nice to remember these times spent together. I usually did not go, however, because I really did not speak enough Spanish to fit in when a lot of people were talking. I tried on occasion, but most of the time, I did not go. Trenton, however, fit right in and always went when he had the chance. On this Independence Day, he was staying with me because Laurel and Lalo had left for the States.

I remember the first time that I heard a mariachi band on my street. I was woken up around 1:00 a.m. by a band playing and men singing. I looked out the door of my living room, and there across the street and down a few houses was my neighbor woman sitting in a chair in the street, and the mariachi band was all around her, serenading her. That was so cool! It happened quite a bit while I was living there at various houses around my neighborhood. I would usually see them as I was out walking the dog or could just hear them from my house and not see them at all. As I sit here in Michigan with my furnace on, I can feel the warm night air, hear the music playing, and put myself there very easily in my mind.

The Beat Goes On

L aurel was gone now, and it was just me running and doing everything. I was a little nervous the first night that she left because we had to pick everyone up at Las Perlas as Hurricane Ivan had damaged the dock at the VCI, and the people could not use it until it was repaired. It happened to be the two four-hour tour day, and I had had ten people scheduled for that morning. Only seven people showed up at Las Perlas, so I had to call and find out what happened. As it turned out, they had been waiting at the VCI dock instead. They claimed that they were never told to come to Las Perlas. I apologized to them, and they ended up going out in the afternoon. This started my time working alone! Luckily, we had plans of pulling the boat out to have it repainted and have fiberglass work done on it once again. Of course this was planned around the time that Laurel would be gone because I just did not want to do all the work by myself. Even though I had stuck Laurel with it many times, I was a lot older and did not want to deal with it.

That next day is when I finally got my truck back. On Monday, September 20, we were supposed to have the boat taken out of the water. During the previous night, Armando had fumigated our house. That morning when I got up, I found Mañana, a rescue puppy of mine that I later renamed Delila, lying on one of the stairway steps foaming at the mouth and drooling. I called the vet and took her right in. She vomited twice on the way there; he gave her two shots to counteract the poison. He told me that they can absorb the poison used for fumigating into the pads of their feet. With her being so little and she had been so sickly when I got her, it did not take much. I took her home and put her in her crate and had to be on my way.

I was supposed to meet the guys at the boat at 9:30 a.m. but was a little late. I went over to Isla Mujeres with the guys and the boat. As it turned out after waiting for several hours, our boat did not get taken out that day. We had to wait until the next day! The man that runs the dry dock over there did not have me written down on their schedule for us to be there. So he had to move some boats already in dry dock to make a space for our boat, and this took some time and some charm and persistence on my part. We ended up spending the whole entire day there, and our boat stayed in the slip overnight where the belts are to lift it out of the water. The next morning, we met at the ferry and went to the island once again. Taking the boat out of the water took three days instead of one! We were already two days behind and planned on being off work for only two weeks total.

On September 26, I received a phone call from Kevin telling me that Laurel and Lalo were stuck in Detroit because Hurricane Jeanne was hitting full force in Florida on the same path as Charley, Frances, and Ivan had hit. There were no planes landing in Florida. They were finally able to fly into Florida and went with Brittnay to sign her up to get into the Job Corps. They arrived back in Cancun on September 29, my birthday. It was a nice birthday present! Believe me, I was very glad to have her back. We had been waiting for the guy that we had contracted with to get the paint for our boat. On October 1, Laurel and I went out to Bonfil to his house to see the paint and make sure on the colors. Of course, as was getting to be very normal but very frustrating, he did not have the paint! We received a call from Palemon that he had received a paper from the harbor master requiring him to report to the office on Isla Mujeres. We had to pick him up and all of us went over to Isla Mujeres to see what the problem was with the harbor master.

Well, we had to pay the fee for pulling our boat out of the water. I had to go to the bank on the island and withdraw 3,800 pesos or US $380 out of my account once again to cover this charge. We had paid it the year previously but had hoped to escape this time. *Not!* We got busted once again! It is such a ridiculous fee. Any boat that is used for tourism has to pay this fee supposedly every time that they have their boat taken out of the water for any repair. Good grief! Saturday, no paint yet! Sunday at the meetings, Laurel and I told everyone that our boat would be in the water and ready for tours once again by Thursday. Monday, no paint! Tuesday, I was on my way back to the states. I was flying home to Michigan, meeting my friends on the expressway, and we were all headed down to Kentucky to the Arabian nationals in Louisville, Kentucky. My girlfriends were taking three Arabs down to show. I was in the States for a total of three weeks, leaving Laurel once again to handle things by herself. There were many problems with the boat getting done on time, problems with the guy that we had contracted with, but the paint job turned out beautifully. Laurel was not able to have a tour on that Thursday; it had to be cancelled. However, the boat was in the water that Friday and ready to go. Once again, we had a pink and purple boat! The only one of its kind; I am sure of it! The top of the deck and hulls were pink also, no white this time around, only pink, purple, and black bottom paint. We finally got the colors that we wanted! Hip, hip, hooray!

After we had the boat pulled out and had $5,000 of work done on her, we were once again very short on money. Things became very rough for us once again. We were behind on the restaurant bill, and we received a notice from the harbor master's office on Isla Mujeres once again. Laurel and I went over on the ferry after the tour had left. We got to the harbor master's office, and they started piddling around with our paperwork and permits. They then told us that they needed to see Palemon. We went to the restaurant hoping to find him there and did. We then all went to the Harbor Master's office once again. We were in there for almost an hour, and poor Palemon got a citation. It was the first one ever on his record of being a captain for fourteen or fifteen years! We felt very bad because of this. They also pointed out to

Palemon that our *turismo nautica* permit was expiring soon and that we should have started applying for it twenty days prior to the expiration date! They "offered" to do the paperwork over there on the island and forgo the late fines and issue the permit for six years for twenty thousand pesos or U.S.$2,000.00. We said that we would have to think about it. We decided to go to the harbor master's office in Puerto Juarez as we had been doing since we started. By now, we had a relationship going with the people there and felt that it would be a mistake to go over to the Island not to mention a great expense. For once, we went with our gut feeling and were much better off having done so. There were no problems at all, and when it was all said and done, we were issued our turismo nautica for ten years to be renewed year by year (which means the price was broken down into ten years instead of having to pay for ten years all up front). Best of all, no fines were ever mentioned nor collected. They were just trying to get a lot of money out of us over on the island. They stopped Palemon quite often and tried to get money or beer from him. That is a normal thing; however, we decided when we started that we were not going to pay any bribes for anything because it was against our principals and we were probably the only all-legal boat running tourists.

I had purchased two new used sails, a mainsail and a genoa, when I was in the States the last time. It cost me almost as much to buy them as it was to have them shipped and the import tax on them! By November 2004, the business owed me $5,000 more of my personal money, which I kept hoping and expecting to eventually get back. My personal account at home was down to $300, so I was pretty much through helping finance things for the business. That means we either make some money, or we will be done. This is how it had gone along since we started getting busy with tours. We were always hanging by a string, not starving, but still not making any money. I had pretty much decided that my personal money was not an option any longer. I had sold off a whole lot more of my mutual funds than I had ever dreamed that

I would ever do or have to do. We were either going to make it on what we took in, or we were going to close up shop. Eventually, the VCI dock was repaired, and we were once again able to pick up our people at the VCI dock. Things were settling down a bit, Brittnay was doing marvelous in the Job Corps, and Thanksgiving was upon us. We were, as usual, still having motor problems. It was an almost everyday occurrence these days. We wanted to buy a new four-stroke twenty-five horsepower in the worst way but could not swing it. So the mechanic kept the thing running as best he could. This had been an ongoing problem almost from the time that we got the boat to Cancun.

On Thanksgiving Day in 2004, we were actually able to buy a turkey. Turkeys are very expensive down there, and we were never able to buy one until this Thanksgiving. It was decided that I would do the cooking (go figure), and Laurel would take care of the tour. I cooked and cleaned all day and then went out to the boat in the afternoon to greet the people. Carol, Cheryl, and Garnet, our friends, had gone out on our boat that day. We invited them to come and share our Thanksgiving dinner with us. Brittnay suggested to me that I should mention one of our dinners and what we ate. She missed her grandma's cooking! I had made homemade pumpkin (that would be right from the cooked pumpkin) pies. However, they did not turn out up to my standards because you cannot buy ginger down there. So I overcompensated for the ginger by using more cloves and cinnamon. My apple pies, however, turned out absolutely wonderful. We had turkey, dressing, mashed potatoes, gravy, millionaire fruit salad, cranberries at $2.20 a can, candied sweet potatoes, green bean casserole, and pies. Are you hungry yet?

Carol, Cheryl, and Garnet were about an hour late, and we figured that they were not coming. Everything was ready to serve; everyone was hungry, so we ate. They finally arrived, and we found out that the taxi driver from the hotel zone did not know where Porto Allegre was. That is the name of the subdivision-type area where I lived. They ate and enjoyed it very much. It was a good day! We had the posada for the guys on December 17 at Laurel's house. We were able to serve turkey again with all the trimmings. We wanted to show the guys and their families what we eat to celebrate Thanksgiving and Christmas in the United States. I had bought Christmas gifts for Palemon's children when I was home in the States the last time. They were a little overwhelmed with all the gifts. The children in general in Mexico only receive one gift at Christmas. They either receive it at Christmas Day or Three Kings' Day, which is twelve days after Christmas if I remember correctly. They do not receive gift after gift after gift even though their parents may be affluent parents. This is their custom, and I think it is great! We had Christmas at Laurel's house that year.

A picture of one of the neighborhoods where Laurel lived.

We were able to give gifts this year; that was a blessing. Things had not been good since my return back to Cancun in October. We had decided to give ourselves one more high season, which is from mid January through April.

Just One More Grand Day in Mexico: January 31, 2005

The business had greatly improved in the last two weeks of January. This Monday evening after the boat had come in from the second tour, I was there early, waiting for the boat to come in. It was quincena, which is payday to us in the United States. Remember, down there, mostly everyone gets paid every fifteen days regardless of what day of the week it falls on. After the boat unloaded, Palemon was ready to start the motor and take off for Las Perlas, where the boat was kept. I stopped him and told him that I had two cases of beer that I would like unloaded from the back of my truck. Walter, our photographer, and Palemon went for the beer, and Pablo was making out the list of supplies needed in the morning. I informed him that we had twenty-five people going out the next day. We were very excited about that! I started walking off the dock when Palemon and Walter were just walking back to the boat with the two cases of beer.

I told Palemon that I wanted him at the boat at 8:15 a.m. for supplies as we were going to have twenty-five people going out. He pretended that he did not hear me, handed the case of beer to Walter, and walked over to me. He reached out and handed me the boat keys and said, "I quit." That was it; he said nothing else!

I just looked at him and told him, "Thanks for the notice." I couldn't believe that this was happening and that he could do such a thing to us. I told him, "I cannot believe that you are doing this, and do remember that what goes around comes around." I then started walking down the dock to the truck. I was flabbergasted to say the least. My mind finally kicked into working order when

I reached the beach, and I realized that I had not had him sign anything to the effect that he quit. I ran back out on the dock, yelling at him above the motor noise to stop and wait! I told him that I needed him to write that he was quitting and sign it.

He said to me, "Why? I am not going to put a demand on you or anything." I told him that if he could not trust me, why should I trust him. You see, after he told me he quit, he told me that he did not give me notice because he thought that I would not pay him for the quincena. This was just an excuse on his part because he knows darn well that I would pay him no matter what happened. Therefore, he did not show any trust. Why would he think of that all of a sudden? Should I be trusting his word? He got off the boat, wrote on a piece of paper that he was quitting, and signed it. He knew exactly what he was doing to us. We needed a new despacho signed by him to turn into the harbor master for February; we had twenty-five people going out the next day that he probably figured we would have to cancel, and it definitely is not easy to find a sailing captain. I called Laurel to inform her of the "great news," and we went from there. We called our dear friend, Carlos, once again for help. We asked him if he knew of any sailing captain that we could possibly get for tomorrow's tour. He gave us a guy's name, Alex, who was a captain for a private boat, and Carlos thought maybe he could help us out. As it turned out, he was able to help us for the rest of the week. We were able to have our tour with the twenty-five people. Thank God!

We decided to have Pablo go to school for his captain's license, and we would pay for it and for getting the license. Pablo started working as our captain, so we then needed a new first mate. God sent us Jose. Right after Palemon had quit as we were standing in the little public parking area where we parked each day for the boat, up walked this guy and started talking to us in Spanish, asking if we were looking to hire a first mate! His name was Jose, and we told him that "Yes, as a matter of fact, we were looking for a first mate." We asked him if he had his papers with him, and no, he did not. So we asked him to come the next day after the boat came in so that our captain could talk to him and look at his paperwork (Another coincidence?). Laurel and I both had a good feeling about Jose right from the very beginning. We felt that this is the guy for us. We hired him after Pablo and Laurel checked over his paperwork, and he started the next week working for us. So now we have Pablo and Jose working for us. All of this time, whenever we needed him, Trenton would work on the boat too. He was getting really good at it and had worked out on the boat the previous summer while on summer break. He liked working on the boat very much, especially when there happened to be teenage girls going out!

He begged to work on the day that our good friend Kevin, once again, called and told us that he was escorting the San Francisco 49ers cheerleaders around Cancun and wondered if we would take them out on our all-day island tour for free. They were in Cancun shooting photos for *Sports Illustrated* swimsuit calendar. We were so excited about the prospect of the girls going out on our boat and honored. We told Kevin that yes we would take them out on a private tour and would foot the bill. Lunch was included on the island as well. We had to cancel some people to open up the day for them, but that was okay with us; we were just so excited to have them. Even Lalo wanted to work on the boat that day! We greeted them in the morning as usual. Kevin took a lot of pictures; Lalo came out with us and took pictures as well, and then they were off.

This is the San Francisco 49er Cheer Leader
tour. Trenton is working on the boat.

San Francisco 49er Cheer Leaders leaving for their tour.
September 2005 right before the hurricane Wilma.

We did get to talk to some of them, and they all seemed very nice. We greeted the boat as usual when they came back from the tour. Everyone had a great time, and we were told by one of the people in charge that our business card logo and info would appear on the calendar. However, to my knowledge, that never happened. The girls had a free tour, free meal, a wonderful time, and not one of them offered to tip our guys. That was very surprising to us and very disappointing to them and us also. Live and learn. That would be our last freebie; you can bet your life on it!

On March 9, 2005, Pablo and his wife, Adriana, had their first child, a boy. They named him Braulio. She had to have him by C-section, which Pablo had been terribly worried and distracted about. He told me that they could not afford this and asked if he could borrow the money from me. I thought it over and talked to our accountant to see if there would be any way that we could deduct a certain amount every quincena from his pay. The accountant told me that this would be possible, so I did lend him the money, not that I had a whole lot to lend at that point in time in my life. I certainly was more able to do so than he was, so I did. After all, Laurel and I had decided a long time ago that we were going to try to be decent employers down there. The day she went in for her C-section, we had a tour scheduled. However, the winds were blowing from the north, and the harbor master closed the port. We sent the guys home, and on Pablo's way home, he received a phone call that she was going into labor, so he was able to be there with her. We had had to cancel nineteen people on that day. The next day, the port was closed again, and we had two private tours that day that we had to cancel.

Sending out a private tour for someone's birthday.

I have written in my journal in March of 2005 that we had our vehicles in and out of the mechanics for quite some time now. At one point, my truck, Laurel's car, and the boat motor were all being worked on at the same time.

My neighborhood-Laurel is working on her car.

On March 15, 2005, I have written:

> Well, the winds are still blowing. We had four people go out yesterday in the morning. We had twelve for the afternoon. However, they had to come back within half an hour into the tour because the port was closed. We had to refund the twelve fares. We had fifteen people the next day that we had to cancel because the port was closed. We not only lost the money for the tour, but most of the time, we did not find out the port was closed until after we had bought the breakfast food and ice for the day, and if it was half day tours, the sandwiches that we made for the people all was for naught. We also had to come up with the $6,000 pesos similar to U.S. $600.00 for our back taxes for the state and city, which our previous accountant failed to tell us that we were supposed to be paying.

Also around this time, Laurel was having more and more problems with Trenton. He was being more and more difficult and doing things that he was not supposed to be doing. Lalo had told Laurel about a school in Puerto Morales that takes the kids all week, and they go home for the weekend. They were going to check this out for Trenton. As it turned out, Trenton ended up going there after Easter break. The school is a public school. The boys can stay there all week; they get three squares a day, and go home on weekends. They have so many hours of school, study time, structured play time, and lights out at a certain time, sort of like the army. The school is right on the Caribbean, and they also teach the boys boating, motor repair, fishing, and things they can do for a living afterward. The first week when we went to pick him up, he had more bruises than he had white skin. His mouth was really getting him into trouble. He finally learned to keep his mouth shut once in a while, learned a little self-discipline, discipline, and that everything was not always going to be Trenton's way. There was a big change in attitude when he would come back for the weekends starting in about two weeks. That was one of the best things that could have happened to him.

March 27, 2005, was Easter Sunday and was also when Braulio was baptized. We all went to the baptism, and then we went to Pablo's mom and dad's house to join the family in celebration. Our friend Carol from Florida came with us also. She had also been to the wedding. When we got there, the music was just blaring, people were everywhere, and we were, once again, treated like family. This time, we were able to sit at the table with Pablo's relatives and actually talk to them. It was a very special time for Pablo and Adriana and for us also.

On April 22, 2005, I have written in my journal:

> My God, my God, why have you forsaken us? I feel like screaming to the heavens! The one stay that has been going for quite some time, when we still had Palemon, is done! It was one of the front stays that connects the two pontoons together in the front under the tramp. We have been trying to get our friend Carlos to get us one from the States for months. He never was able to get it made; therefore, it was not replaced until now. I found out that we could order one through one of the boat supply stores that we dealt

with all the time. They told me when I ordered it that, "It would be here in a few days." We had placed the order for it the previous week after having to cancel tours first because the port was closed and then because of the stay. The next week, the stay was supposed to be in on Monday, so we did not book a tour until Wednesday. We ended up having to cancel two four-hour tours that day because the stay still was not in. On Thursday of that week, we had scheduled twenty-five people for the island tour. We still had no stay.

We did some scrambling and rented the Crusario for the day for 5,000 similar to U.S. $500.00 pesos plus IVA (this is a tax). The Crusario is a big wooden boat, which looks like a pirate ship sort of but on a smaller scale. Pablo's father is the captain of this boat. When the boat arrived in the morning to pick up our people (they were expecting our thirty-six feet catamaran), everyone was pretty much okay with the different boat except one family. Laurel and I explained to everyone what was going on and why we were using this boat instead of ours. We offered to give the one family that were not too happy their money back, but they decided to go. We then went to the Royal Sands after the boat left to give the Thomas Moore reps there a heads up on the people that were not too happy. The minute the people of this particular family got off the boat, they went to the Thomas Moore rep and complained about the tour after having had the entire tour, eating lunch, and drinking all day on the boat. They ended up getting 50 percent of their tour refunded, which means that we got the shaft! The rep told us that this family complains about something every year, so they are pros at it.

The next day, we had a private tour that we had to cancel because the stay was not in yet! The people were very nice about it and said that they would try us again next year. I kept going into the boat store and inquiring about our stay. We were finally informed that it was being held up in customs at the airport. Finally, on the following

Monday, we received the stay! We lost two weeks total of work because of the port being closed and not getting the stay in on time. All of the time, of course, we had to pay our guys' wages.

Time was passing, but the business was not getting any better or worse, kind of staying status quo. When I had gone back to the states, I had taken our tour information along with brochures. I had visited all the travel agencies in my hometown plus the nearby town which is a lot higher in population. As I spoke with the travel agents at these agencies about our tour, I asked if they could possibly recommend or at least let their people know about us who were planning a trip to Cancun. I got nothing but positive responses from the agents verbally. However, we never once got a booking from any of their people that had come down. I also had tried to get my local newspaper to write an article about us and about what we had accomplished a couple of different times. However, I was never able to peak their interest. You would think that being the only two women from the United States to do what we had done would be of interest to my hometown newspaper. At least, that is what I thought! Well, I thought wrong; they were not interested. I guess if maybe I had committed crimes down there, then they might have been interested. It is not that we did not try to get the word out; we tried every way that we could imagine. We tried to get into Apple, thinking that because they were Americans and we were also Americans, which would count for something. *Not!* We tried to get into Fun Jet and every other large travel agency down there. No luck. So we were still only being sold by the five Royals and a couple of Internet travel agencies in Cancun plus our website.

In June of 2005, it was time for Brittnay to return home to us from the Job Corps. She had opted for her GED instead of getting her high school diploma. She had also talked of continuing on and getting an associate degree at some point in time of her stay there. However, she was very anxious to get back to Cancun and to her family. The day that she was flying in was very exciting for us and her. She would soon be eighteen, and we had not seen her in over a year! When she walked out to us, she was wearing a business suit and high heels and looked very grown up. She had an entirely different attitude and was ready to face the world. We were very proud of her.

I went back home to Michigan in July to ride, visit, and relax. While I was there, Cancun had her first hurricane of the season. Laurel was handling everything so of course had to deal with this also. They were under hurricane warnings, and our guys, Pablo and Jose, were supposed to take the boat over to Isla Mujeres on Wednesday. The hurricane was supposed to hit on Friday. On that Wednesday afternoon, Pablo called Jose and told him that he was going to move the boat on Thursday morning instead and never bothered to call Laurel. Remember, he is the captain; Laurel is the owner. Laurel heard from Jose on this, so she called Pablo to find out what the problem was. He said that he was not feeling well but not to worry since he would be there at the boat on Thursday morning to move her. Then on Wednesday around midnight, Laurel received a phone call from Adrianna, Pablo's wife, stating that Pablo was too sick and would not be at the boat on Thursday morning but could be there Thursday afternoon. After Pablo got married and had a baby, I just knew that he would be a problem when and if a hurricane came. I had said as much to Laurel previous to this situation.

Anyway, Laurel went out to the boat at 1:00 p.m. on Thursday and no Pablo. She called him, and he said that there was no way he would be able to move the boat. She told him that he had to come and move the boat he was under contract, and there was no one else to move the boat! He refused to come and hung up on her. She tried to call him back, but he would not answer his phone. Laurel called Captain Manuel, a captain that we had used in the past as an emergency; he came right out to the boat, and Manuel, Jose, and Laurel took the boat over to Isla Mujeres and just tied her up the best that they could.

Laurel returned to Cancun and called Pablo once again. She told him he had better report to her in Puerto Juarez on Friday and go over to Isla Mujeres with her and Jose and help get the boat ready for the hurricane. She also told him to bring a report from the doctor stating what was wrong with him, and that he had indeed gone to the doctor being so sick and all. When he met her the next day at the Ferry, he handed her a handwritten note stating that he was still too sick to work and could not bring the boat back to Cancun after the hurricane. The note stated that he had a temperature of 105 degrees! When she received the note from him, she did not say anything and tucked it away in a safe place. He did take the ferry over to Isla Mujeres with her and Jose.

However, when he got over there, he went into the OXXO (it is like a 7-Eleven store), bought something minor like a bottle of soda, took the receipt and wrote on the back of the slip that he quit. He then took the next ferry back to Cancun. Laurel and Jose went to the boat, retied her, took off the rudders, and stowed them below, took the motor off and stowed that, took off the boom and stowed that, and called it good. She and Jose then came back to Cancun on the ferry to wait out the hurricane. Remember, this is the same Pablo who had been with us two weeks after the boat arrived in Cancun. The same guy whom we had paid weekly through thick and thin. The same guy that we let go early many, many days plus the days that he did not even have to report to work but got paid. The same guy whom I had just lent money to for his wife's C-Section. Yes, our "dear" Pablo.

During the time that Jose and Laurel were getting the boat prepared for the hurricane, Jose had told Laurel about all the gas that Pablo had been stealing from us, almost daily. After we would bring in the gas containers in the morning and drop them off at the boat, instead of Pablo putting the gas in the boat, he would tell Jose to run it up to shore and put the gas into his (Pablo's) car. I had been asking and asking, "Why are you using so much gas when this is a sailing tour?" Well, now we knew! There had been other things that he had been stealing off the boat as well. After the hurricane, as Laurel and Jose were preparing to go over to the island and get the boat, Pablo showed up to go and get her. He had already given Laurel the note quitting, so she waited until the boat was back in Cancun and docked before she asked him for the keys to the boat. He looked at her and asked her why. She told him that he had quit the other day. He left the boat after having given her the keys and ran right down to the federal building and put a demand on us stating that we had fired him! Once again, déjà vu! Cesar all over again.

The two good friends had both managed to screw us. We had not seen that one coming. Once again, we are without a captain. Not only without a captain, but I had no way of collecting the money that I had loaned him for his new baby. I was still in Michigan and did try to check my e-mail daily except when I was up north trail riding on my horse. I received an e-mail stating that Pablo had quit. *Great!* Now what?

When I returned to Cancun, Laurel had found a captain by the name of Caprice. He was a character. Let me tell you. He was a really nice guy, but there was something about him that just wasn't right, if you know what I mean. He worked for us while we put an AD in the paper looking for another captain. In the meantime, there was a captain of a dive boat that worked out of the same dock we were working out from. He wanted to know if we would consider him as a captain. We really did not want him as our captain because we had known him for a while now and never were very impressed with his character. We didn't quite know how to handle this situation, so we offered him a lot less money than we normally paid our workers. Well, his boss got wind of this deal—his boss was the same guy that told us there was no dock space when we were looking for a new place to move our boat. This just set him off against us once again! Go figure! We were not even after his captain; the captain was after us!

We had one captain come out for an interview and to show us what kind of sailor he was in a Speedo! He was a Zen-type person, kind of unusual, great sailor...but...we proceeded to inform him that he would have to wear our uniform, which consists of tan Bermuda-type shorts and a company polo shirt, no Speedo. We never heard from him again, thank goodness! I take that back; he did try to date Laurel for a while, kept calling her up and asking her out. Boy, sure glad we followed our first instincts on that one! We had Caprice for quite some time. He was a baseball nut and played minor baseball and also coached a women's slow-pitch team. Laurel and I both had played women's slow-pitch in the states, and Brittnay had played girls baseball. She was an excellent catcher. *Hmm*, I had been the catcher on my women's team. That or first base. Anyway, Caprice told us we should come to a practice. *So* we did. That went over like a lead balloon. Three white women on an all-Mexican women's softball team. I only went to a couple of practices, and that was enough for me. Laurel and Brittnay continued practicing with them; however, when it came time for the games, women would show up for the game that they had never seen at a practice and get to play while they sat at the bench. That did not go on for too long, and Laurel and Britt had both had enough too. Of course, this was after I had made a trip to the States and bought Laurel a new softball glove. Oh well, another lesson in life.

We had one captain show up for an "interview," which consisted of taking our boat out on a tour. We had people scheduled that day; he showed up, couldn't get the motor started, and walked away. He told us he couldn't work under those conditions. We needed a new motor so badly but could not afford one. Needless to say, we had to cancel that tour. We continued with Caprice and kept trying to talk Jose into becoming our captain. Caprice had been teaching him the whole entire time that he had been working for us. We offered to pay for schooling for Jose, and he finally accepted. He had to sign up for a class and find out when they were going to offer another one. In the meantime, we finally acquired a new captain by the name of Miguel. Miguel was a very sweet older man, a very good captain but getting up there in age and had a problem a lot of times remembering things. He was a very kind man and good sailor, but he did not speak much English. Therefore, he had a hard time communicating with our clients. Jose, our first mate, did not speak much English either. We were muddling through all this when we heard the news of a hurricane coming named Wilma.

Hurricane Wilma

It is October of 2005. There is a hurricane coming, supposedly to make a direct hit on Cancun. Once again, déjà vu. We watched and waited and listened to the harbor master weather reports and warnings. It is a Thursday morning, and she is definitely coming! We went to the boat early in the morning with my truck. We unloaded everything stored on the boat such as all the snorkeling gear for thirty people, life jackets, all the sails, everything. I took everything home to my house, and Laurel, Jose, Armando, and the captain at that time, Caprice, left the dock and headed for Isla Mujeres shortly thereafter. They got to the island, found a good place in the mangroves in the inlet, and tied *The Pollo Primavera* up. They took the boom down and off, took off the motor, took off one rudder, and couldn't get one of the rudders off, and they stored everything below in one of the hauls as safely as possible. They tied the hatches down as best they could, tied her up as best they could, said a prayer, and left her. They took the ferry back to Cancun.

By then, since we had had the experience of the last big hurricane that was supposed to hit, Laurel's children and I had gone shopping at the grocery store and filled both autos up with gas. This all took place Thursday morning. We got lucky; no one believed yet that the hurricane was coming. We were able to stock up on water, food, everything that we wanted. I had gone across the street and asked my neighbors if they needed anything as I was going to the grocery store, and not all of them had a car. They wanted to know if there really was going to be a hurricane. I said, "Yes, and it is going to be a big and bad one." They told me no; they did not really need anything. So I went and shopped for Armando and me. When I got back to the house, Armando was home. We then went out to Jose's house. He lived way out in the northern part of Cancun where the very poor lived. The road that he lived on was indescribable to the normal person who has never experienced any such thing. I used to think that Palemon lived way out, but his place was nowhere near where Jose lived. He lived out by the army base and all the night clubs that had strippers and such.

Anyway, the road that he lived on would not be drivable with a regular car. I was very glad that I had a four-wheel drive truck every time that I went down there. Jose lived in one of those stick houses with tar paper roofs. I took everything they had of value, such as their TV, radio, and not much more. I took him, his wife, and son into town to their other house that he owned. They were going to stay there to weather out the hurricane. We then went home. Laurel, Lalo, and the kids were at their house. Armando, Fargo, and I were in mine. I took a tarp and wrapped it around the outside of my air conditioner and used bungee cords to tie it down. Armando unhooked the gas tank and brought it into the back porch-type area and tied it down. I had two palm trees in pots that we brought inside also. We had everything that we could think of tied down. Armando even took a rope and tied around the cap of my truck to try to protect that.

By Thursday night, we had lost all communication with each other (Laurel and I); we had no electricity, and later in the evening, I lost the cover over the skylight that I had on my roof. The water on Thursday evening was building up in the back so high that it started running through the house and out the front door. When the cover blew off the skylight, I had a waterfall running down my stairway. Before it all started, I had taped all the windows and took most of the furniture upstairs along with the things that I had brought from Jose's house. Armando had had me fill a garbage can and all the containers that I had with water for flushing toilet and washing. I had bought five garrafons of drinking water. When it got dark, we lit candles for a while and played the game Racko.

By the time that we went to bed, the rain was coming in the windows so hard, you could put a beach towel up against the windowpane; five minutes later, the towel would be soaked. The only way to soak up water was to put towels down, soak up the water, squeeze the towel out in a bucket, and throw it out. This I had to keep doing upstairs to try to keep the things dry that were upstairs. Downstairs, there was no chance. By Thursday night, I had two inches of water on all the floors in the downstairs area. Fargo, at night, lay in two inches of water to sleep. I had no couch, only two chairs, and he could not fit in either one of those. Friday came; the wind was indescribable! I stood at the door and watched my neighbor's roof of their carport blow away tile by tile down the street.

Everyone lost their TV dish that was installed on their roof. I ended up with one on my roof hanging down over and clanging into my spare bedroom window upstairs. There wasn't much to do, but I tried to read, play cards or Racko, or talk and listen to the wind and watch the "river" running though the house. On Friday night, as we lay in bed, we could feel the house shake. This house was made of cement blocks, angel iron running up through the cement blocks, and each house had it's own cement blocks built up to each other. Honestly, we could feel the house shaking. As I lay in my bed, feeling the house shake, hearing the wind like you have never heard it before unless you have been in a hurricane, seeing the rain hit the windows and seep around the window frames, I thought that I was going to drown in my bed. I could also hear the Caribbean both Friday and Saturday nights with the waves crashing in. We lived several miles from the Caribbean, but I still thought that I was going to drown. On Saturday morning, the wind subsided and the rain stopped and we thought that the hurricane was over. The next thing that

I knew, Laurel, Lalo, and the kids were at my door to see if we were okay. I could not believe that she drove her car all the way over to my house to see if I was okay. I do not know how she got through all the flooded streets, electric poles downed, and everything that was in the streets. She did, however, and I was sure happy to see her.

We chitchatted for a while, and then Armando and I took them back in my truck because she did not want to try and drive her car back, and I didn't want her to either. What a trip it was! There was about two feet of water in all the streets, and in the bad spots, the water was up to the hood of my truck. There were cement electric poles down all over; the gas stations and convenient stores were all blown apart, away, down, you name it. It looked as if we had been bombed! We got back to her house, and I dropped them off. Her front window was blown out, and her leg got cut by blowing glass when that happened. They had water pouring into the house through the light sockets! The computer and computer desk were ruined for one thing. There was so much damage. We just got safely back home and into the house, and the wind started all over again. That had been the eye of the hurricane going over. That lasted six hours.

By Sunday afternoon, once again, the rain and the wind stopped; the sun came out, and Wilma had left us. Thank God! We were still all in one piece, and the kids were all out playing in the water in the street. It was like one big swimming pool. The water was okay until the sewer systems started backing up into the rainwater. Then you did not want to walk in it. Fargo was finally able to go outside and go to the bathroom. On Saturday night, I had decided that we were going to pick him up and put him in bed with us. He was soaking wet but would not settle down in the bed. That was not his place to be, and he knew it. We put him back down on the floor in the water; I got out some of the boat cushions and laid them down on the floor, wanting him to try and lay on those. He walked into the center of them and started urinating. The poor boy really had to go. After that, he lay on the floor in the water and slept. He did not want to come back up on the bed with us, so that is where I left him to sleep.

Once again, I was praying that we would not drown. When Wilma finally left us, everyone came out of their houses to see what had happened exactly. We soon found out that Hurricane Wilma had been the strongest and longest hurricane in the history of keeping track of hurricanes. Glory be and praise be to God she was gone! All of my neighbors were okay; everyone's houses were still standing in my neighborhood. We lost a lot of trees; of course, all the power lines were down, but we were okay. Fargo, once again, was able to go outside and go to the bathroom. The poor ole guy had held his bowels for three days! What a relief it was to be able to take him for a walk and let him relax a bit.

By Monday, Armando and I were able to drive over to Laurel's house to see how they were. The devastation was unbelievable. There was a gas station/convenience store very near their house that was being pilfered as we drove by with onlookers standing around laughing. It was very sad to watch something like that. I had never seen anything like this in my entire life! I had come from a reasonably small rural-type town where everyone pretty much trusted everyone else, especially in the area that I lived. We got to Laurel's house, and everyone was fine. We decided to take a drive and look things over. They were not allowing anyone into the hotel zone yet, and there were no ferryboats allowed to run to Isla Mujeres yet either.

We drove around the area just looking in amazement. Along Bonampak Avenue, there were big heavy cement light poles that were almost all snapped off and lying down like some giant had walked through with his arms out and knocked them all down. It was amazing!

The devastation of hurricane Wilma.

Results of Wilma.

Hurricane.

Hurricane.

This is a picture of the ferry that was blown ashore
in Puerto Juarez, described in the book.

The back of Plaza Las Americas Mall was totally in ruins. The
Sears store was pretty much demolished. The hospital next door
to that was in shambles or gone. All of this was a couple of miles
away from where my house was. The streets were pretty much all
flooded, and the neighborhood people were all out, trying to clear
the gutters and sewer covers, trying to get the water to drain into
the sewers as best that they could. Where there were sewer covers
missing, most of those big holes had trees or tree limbs sticking
out of them so that no one would drive into them. I was one of
the few who had a truck, so there were not a lot of people out
driving around.

By the next day, we were allowed into the hotel zone. Oh my,
what a shock! All of the jungle was gone! You could only see brown
sticks sticking out at random. Most of the hotels were pretty much
destroyed. The place where we had kept our boat was pretty much
in ruins with not much dock left at all. There had been a restaurant
built on the water connected to the dock—that was gone. The sand
was piled up and through a lot of the floors and pool. The water

was so murky, and stuff was floating everywhere. As we continued down through the hotel zone, we were in awe of the power of God! The brand-new hotel that Brittnay had been working in was pretty much gone. It had been built mostly of glass; and once the glass started breaking, the wind just took over! The only hotels that sustained without much damage were the Royal Resorts.

A few days after the hurricane, we were finally able to take a ferry across to Isla Mujeres to see if we had a boat. Deep down in my heart, I was hoping that we did not! Things had been such a struggle for so long, and I had decided that I no longer wanted to live in Mexico before Wilma came along. I had decided that whether or not the business succeeded, I was leaving and going back to Michigan in June. Laurel could do what she wanted— either stay and run the business or we would try to sell the business, and she could come back to Michigan with me. Once I had decided this, I mulled it over for about three weeks before I expressed my thoughts with Laurel. She had decided to stay and run the business without me. Now, if we no longer had a boat, the decision would be made for us both.

Laurel, Trenton, Armando, and I took the ferry over to the island. The island really had not sustained as much damage as Cancun. However, all the main roads were covered in sand. They were being bulldozed, and dump trucks were loaded with sand when we arrived. There were hardly any busses running, but we managed to catch a bus and go to the end of the route that they had. From there, we had to start walking and trying to find where Laurel and Armando thought that they had left the boat. It was very difficult to tell because everything was destroyed and nothing looked the same. After Armando went through the jungle and the swamps without finding the boat, we started walking around the swampy area that he had just been in. Laurel and I could hear the halyards clanging on the masts of some of the boats. We could also see the top of some of the masts. We just had to find a way to get to them.

We finally walked to the other side of the slip and found a dock with a boat tied to it with the owner on board. We asked if we could walk out on the dock and onto his boat to see if we could see our boat. He gave us permission, and we went out and looked around. Across the slip in the mangroves stood our boat. The boat tied up right next to ours was flipped sideways and was sinking. Our boat, however, was absolutely fine. I didn't know whether to cheer or cry! Now that we knew that we still had a boat, it was time to try to get back to the ferry. The ferryboats were only running until 5:00 p.m. because there was still so much debris floating in the seas and you wouldn't be able to see it after dark. By the time we worked our way around the slip of water and tried to catch another bus, it was getting later by the minute. We were getting pretty desperate, and we were on the opposite end and side of the island that we needed to be to catch the ferry. We tried to get a bus, but that became an impossible option. We started walking/running and hurrying the best that we could. Sometimes, we were walking in some pretty ugly looking water. Needless to say, our shoes were all soaked, and at some points, the water was at least a couple of feet deep.

When we finally got to the ferryboat dock, we found out that the last ferry had left for the day along with about one hundred other people that were waiting. Laurel and I had to go to the bathroom so bad by this time, and of course, there was absolutely nothing open. We ended up breaking into a locked outhouse sort of thing and using it! We got back to the dock, and all the people that were still waiting for a ferry were getting pretty restless. Laurel started crying by this time; we were all pretty much at the end of our ropes. Finally, one of the harbor master employees called the harbor master and explained about all of us still waiting for a ferry. There were no hotels, restaurants, and taco stands open on the island. We did not have jackets or sweaters with us, and it was getting chilly by this time.

The harbor master finally gave permission for another boat to run and take us back to Cancun! Glory hallelujah! We got back to Cancun safe and sound and were very glad to be there. By this time, we had not been working for a week. However, our employees were expecting to be paid. When our first mate, Jose, and his family were able to make their way out to my house, they showed up in force expecting to be paid. The roof had been blown totally off their house, and all was lost. By this time, there was no tar paper to be had in all of Cancun. One of my neighbors had a housing supply–type business, and Trenton was a very good friend of theirs. They had been taking him to school every morning all school year. So he went over and asked the señor if he could get us some tar paper for Jose's roof. I ended up paying for it when it came in and delivered it out to Jose's house for him.

During the time that we were not running tours, I was only able to pay our guys half of their pay, which is half more than most of the workers in Cancun were getting at the time because nothing was open, so no one was working or getting paid. Trenton did not have school as there was not a school left where he had been going out in Puerto Juarez. The whole school was filled with sand. He got an offer from a neighbor of theirs to go to Cozumel to work putting up dry wall. He was fifteen years old at that time; he went over there with his neighbor, worked six days, and returned home for one. He stayed right at the jobsite, ate what was available, and earned some money. He was the only one in our family working, not including Armando. Armando got a job offer working as security on our street.

After the hurricane, 175,000 people were out of work of the 1,000,000 people living in Cancun. There was robbery everywhere. A couple of nights after the hurricane, some guys were spotted on the rooftops of our street, looking to rob someone that was not home. All of the men in our neighborhood went out trying to catch the guys, but they got away. After that, a vigilance group was formed by the guys and women on my street. They were taking turns staying out on the street, patrolling. This went on for about a week, and they then decided as more and more went back to work that they could no longer keep this night job up along with their day jobs. So they all decided to hire a night security guard. I informed my neighbor that lived across from me and down a couple of houses that Armando had been working as security guard for twelve years and was out of a job. She was "the mother" of the whole street. She called a meeting of the people of my street, and they decided to hire Armando. That was a godsend for him as he had not been working since Wilma.

Trenton worked over in Cozumel for a total of two weeks. When he came home, he decided that he was old enough to go out and live on his own, quit school, and work full time doing dry wall. He ran away from home; luckily, he didn't go very far and moved in with a friend of his and his mother. Laurel was able to track him down, got him in the car, and informed him that if he did not continue to go to school in Puerto Juarez, she was going to send him to a school in Veracruz. This school in Veracruz is for boys that no longer want to live at home and is run like a reform school. The boys are locked in and are only allowed to return home once a month for a day. Well, he decided very quickly to continue to go to school in Puerto Juarez when it reopened. She was not about to lose another child to the streets of Cancun!

Two weeks after Wilma, the Harbor Master opened the port up to boats once again, and we were able to go over to Isla Mujeres and get our boat and bring her back to Cancun. We had spoken with the manager of Las Perlas, and he was going to allow us to bring our boat back and dock it to what was left of the dock. At the time that we brought our boat back, we were about the only company who had brought our boat back to Cancun. The reason that we wanted to get her back so soon was we were afraid of leaving her sit there not knowing what was happening to her and what was being taken off her or whatever. Everyone in the boat business knew that the *Pollo Primavera* was ours and that we were Americans, which made us fair game for anything.

We got her back, and shortly thereafter, about another week or so, we were being asked by the Thomas Moore people when we were going to start running tours again. Since the Royal Resorts were the only hotels that were able to have tourists stay in them since they did not have hardly any destruction, Thomas Moore was the only travel agency with tourists, which meant that we were the only tourist boat that would have tourists. The VCI dock was totally gone; Las Perlas had been doing construction on their dock, so we were able to get our people on the dock and on our boat. We started serving our continental breakfast on the public beach next door to Las Perlas and then walking the people down the beach to the dock and to our boat. The first week after we were up and running with tours, we had our best week that we had had the whole entire year. When we would see a tourist get off the bus, we knew they were ours because the Royals were the only hotels that had tourists.

The second week of running after Wilma was good but not as good as the first week for us. Soon, the other boat companies had repaired their docks and boats, and they started running with tours also. We continued to struggle along and put up with all the reconstruction going on at Las Perlas. It was getting harder and harder for our boat to get in and out of the dock area because we were being shoved closer and closer to the shoreline. The owner of Las Perlas had brought his big cruiser in and took our dock space, which meant that we had to get closer in. Our boat only drew three feet of water, but when you put tourists on it, you do need to draw more. So we were not only dealing with not enough water to move the boat, but we still had the darn temperamental motor that we kept dealing with.

Our captain was still Capi (Miguel), and he suggested that we start looking for another dock to dock our boat. By now, everyone was building or rebuilding new docks. We made a deal with one of the owners to be able to come and pick up our people there at his dock and were still keeping our boat at Las Perlas. Pretty soon, we were hardly busy with clients at all. One of the other boat owners whom had been friendly toward us in the past approached us about renting our boat out to him when he had too many clients to take all on his boat. We started doing this—supplying our boat, our crew, and our supplies, and he paid us a certain amount per person that he would put on our boat. Pretty soon, he was trying to get us to move our boat to the dock where he had his boat docked. He tried to get the owner of the hotel where his boat was docked to give us permission to dock there, but that never happened.

We did, however, approach the owner of a place right next door who had just built a huge dock and had lots of space. He was in the process of building a night club on the beach and did have bathroom facilities and a room where we could serve our continental breakfasts. Eventually, a contract was worked out with him, and we moved our boat from Las Perlas to the new docking area, which was right next to the company that had been renting our boat. This went on for a few months. The owner of the other company was approaching us now about buying our boat from us. At this time, we were really not interested in selling, but we did talk to him.

Meeting Maná

If you will remember at the beginning of my story, I was telling you about Laurel and my favorite singing group, Maná, and the kids and us singing to the CD. On December 14, 2005, I had taken out all my Christmas CDs and decided to play my Maná CDs for some reason. I got to thinking to myself that now that I was leaving Mexico, I probably would never have the chance to see Maná in concert. Laurel and I had talked previously of when we had money of going to DF Mexico to see them in concert. I had been talking to God and had mentioned the fact that I would never see this group in concert. That very same day Laurel came over and said to me, "I have some very exciting news for you, Mom." She told me that she had heard on the radio that they were giving away free tickets to see Maná that night in Cancun! When we went to greet the boat, we went to look at where they were setting up for the concert. It was in the middle right by the big flag. We decided to drive in early, bringing chairs, a blanket, and cooler, and waited, sort of like going to see the Fourth of July fireworks!

Well, anyway, Laurel, Lalo, and the kids came for me around 6:00 p.m. They stopped at the Oxxo and got some snacks and pop. We then headed out for the hotel zone and the concert area. When we got to the Bull Ring, the roads were being blocked by many, many busses and the police. We drove out to the hotel entrance, and that was totally blocked by the police. Lalo and Trenton got out of the car and went over to the police to ask how to get through to the hotel zone. They told them that if we wanted to get through to go through the back side of the

Bull Ring. Laurel drove around, and we got through that way even though it was partially blocked off and no one was actually supposed to drive through. We got into the hotel zone as far as the Carosel Hotel, and then the police were checking for tickets to the concert. Of course, we didn't have any, so we parked the car and started walking. We got as far as the top of the bridge, and the police were checking for tickets again. Trenton told them we were staying at the Royal Sands, so they let us through. For once, being an American paid off!

We made our way up to where the stage was, and we sat on the curb for a while. First, the police made all the Mexicans leave the area, and then they finally told us to leave also. We then went across the street and stood by the fence. After awhile, we were told we had to go behind the ropes across the street. While we had been sitting on the curb, Lalo took Laurel, and they went for a walk. When they returned, they had actually went to buy me a T-shirt with Maná on it! I was thrilled! I wanted to stand where Maná were supposed to arrive. While we were standing and waiting there, a woman walked up with four VIP tickets and asked if we would like them! Of course, we said yes, and I could hardly keep from jumping up and down as I took them from her. We asked her if we could get one more as Lalo had left our area and was off wandering around. Trenton went off to find Lalo in the thousands of people there, and us women stood jumping up and down like a bunch of teenagers! We were so thrilled and blessed! We went in and sat twelve rows from the center stage. It was absolutely fantastic, a dream come true!

They sang for about two hours, and we were standing there, singing along to all the songs with all the Mexicans in Spanish like we were one of them. For those two hours, we were! God is amazing! When we left, we left shortly before the last song was completed. We were able to walk directly to our car and drive right out of the hotel zone with no problems or traffic jams as most of the people had been bussed in so therefore had to be bussed out. It was handled very nicely and very orderly.

We spent our fourth Christmas in Cancun with both my ceiling fans and Fargo's floor fan running full blast. That is a really weird thing when you come from Michigan, believe me, and you don't ever get used to it. I knew, as well as everyone else, that this would be my last Christmas living in Cancun. I had tried not to tell Armando of my decision to leave until after Christmas, but I just could not keep it from him any longer. Sometime before Christmas, I had told him that I could no longer stand to live in Mexico and that in June, if not sooner because of the business, I would be leaving. It was a very hard thing to do, but I had to do it. He, of course, could not understand and never really did up to the day that I left. Things were never the same between us after I told him that I was leaving. They were very strained at times. It is hard to carry on like everything is okay when you know deep down inside that they are not and that someday soon you will no longer be together. We had a good Christmas, and everyone enjoyed their gifts that I had brought back from my last trip home. By March of 2006, we were trying to sell the business as a business and not break it up. The owner of the company that had been renting our boat was trying to buy our boat. However, his American partner was then going through a divorce and could not swing buying another boat at that time. So that option fell through, surprise!

The north winds were blowing; tours were being cancelled one after another. Laurel and I had not been able to cash a paycheck from the business since the middle of February. Things were going downhill fast, and we could not figure out what was going on with the Thomas Moore reps. We finally went to the head of Thomas Moore and asked for a meeting with the reps. We could not even afford to take in pizza for them. We talked with all of them and told them what was going on—no customers. We asked if there had been complaints that we did not know about or problems with us. Everyone said, "No, there were no problems." We left the meeting kind of shaking our heads and trying to figure out what in the world was going on. We were hardly running any tours by March, going out with two to four people. We finally told them that we would no longer run a tour for two or less people.

Trenton, shortly after the meeting, was in for the meetings on Sunday. He finally nailed down one of the reps and asked him what was going on. He tried to tell Trenton nothing was going on, but Trenton would not let that answer fly. He said, "Come on, my mom and my grandma know that there is something going on that they do not have clients any more." The rep finally admitted that the other boat company was paying each rep $5 per head for everyone that they put on their boats instead of ours. At this point, we could not compete with that. No way! We then made the decision that March 31; it was going to be our last day. I would leave by April 16 for the States. As soon as we had made the decision, we let our guys know what was going on. They were sad to hear the news, but in their hearts, they had to have known that this was coming. We struggled through the last two weeks and had informed Thomas Moore of our decision as well. We were also telling our people as they got off the boat that we would no longer be running after March 31.

As luck would have it, our dear friends through the Royals, Carol, Cheryl, and Garnett were down in Cancun on our last week of running. They went out on our boat as much as possible, and I had a Mexican dinner planned for the last day. On the last day, we did not take any tourists out. Only our friends were invited and family. Armando had decided to move out of my house and into his own place two weeks before I was leaving Cancun. We had a huge argument that morning of our last day, and he ended up not going out with us for our last sail. When I got home that night with all our friends in tow to eat, he had packed up and moved out, leaving me a little note saying good-bye. When the tour ended, we had to bid our guys good-bye and pay them their last money. Our accountant had figured out what they were due for their finiquitos and their last weeks' pay. We not only had to come up with their final weeks' pay, but everyone gets a finiquito when they are let go. It is based upon their pay plus the months of work. That was a very sad moment for Laurel and me.

We stood at my truck, had the guys sign their paperwork, and handed them their last envelopes from us. Laurel and I stood there and cried like babies. We felt so bad that we could not do more for our guys. We told them that when we sold the boat, we would give them a bonus. At that time, we truly thought that we would be able to sell the boat. When I got home that night with all our friends, my house was empty. I started crying once again and then had to make dinner for everyone and try to put on a happy face. Lalo and his brother Veloice ended up making most of the meal. Everything turned out very good, and everyone had a good time. I, on the other hand, had lost another love of my life and a business all in one day! It was time to move on.

Laurel was going to start working for a company within the Royal Resorts, and I was getting ready to leave. Armando, who I had planned on driving with me through Mexico, was no longer going to do so. Laurel kept on insisting that Trenton could do this with me and take a bus back to Cancun. That is eventually how it happened. I still had the hole in the ceiling where the sunlight had been on my roof. My landlord had never repaired it, so Trenton had blocked it as best that he could. It still leaked every time it rained; therefore, there was a rust spot on a few of the steps leading to my upstairs. I had to start packing, and I had to have the air conditioner taken out of the bedroom and have the cement wall repaired. I got Armando to find someone to take out the air conditioner and repair the wall. He then mudded it for me inside and out. He went with me to find paint for the outside of the house, and I bought paint for the inside as well. I had to paint all of the walls because I had lived there for two years and did not want to leave the house in disarray. Wherever Fargo had rubbed up against the walls, there was a black streak.

Even though I had washed Fargo every week, it is very dirty down there. The wind blows so much; I never shut my windows nor my doors, so there was a constant breeze blowing through my house. There is always fine coral on the floors and outside plus the dirt in the streets. It was impossible to keep him clean for longer than a day if that. One day as I was washing him outside my house in the street with my hose, there was a car sitting down the street. The person in the car sat there in his car and watched me wash my dog for almost the entire time that I was washing him. He then drove his car down, stopped in front of me, and proceeded to yell at me for using water to wash my dog. I asked him what he suggested that I use instead of my hose, and he said a bucket. Fargo weighed 130 pounds. Can you imagine how I would wash him with a bucket of water? That is the kind of thing that happened to me all the time. There was always someone yelling at me about my dogs! This guy did not even live on my street nor had I ever seen him before or since the incident. Anyway, that is why I had to repaint all my walls because of Fargo, and the dirty air and streets caused him to be constantly dirty. When I painted the outside of the house, even though I had used the same color as the house, it was much darker because the house had not been painted since it had been new. The old paint faded a lot, so my new dark paint was very outstanding. I painted a huge circle and wanted to put lines all the way around the circle like a picture of the sun, but I didn't. I do not know what the owner of the house thought when he looked at it, but I guess he should have kept in contact with me to know what exactly was going on. I never did see him again nor his mother. He collected the rent for March in the beginning of March, and that was it.

Ruth and Fargo in her kitchen.

As I was getting ready to move, Laurel and the kids moved back in with me for a bit because she and Lalo were in the process of moving from one place to another and had to wait for the new apartment to be cleaned out. So I had three extra people living with me plus all their stuff. By April 9, we were starting to move some of her belongings over to the new place. My favorite neighbors next door to me had moved out by now also. They bought a new and bigger house in another brand-new subdivision where Fargo and I used to walk in the jungle. It was no longer a jungle but had new houses. These people had been really good neighbors, and I missed them. I was very glad to be moving away from the new neighbors that bought the house. They had a schnauzer that barked all night long!

When we stopped running tours and put the business to sleep, we were three months behind on our payments to our accountants. We owed the attorney from the last demanda from Pablo, we had back taxes to pay, and that was it. We were current on the restaurant and the dock. We were still owed for the last two weeks of tourists from Thomas Moore, which would pay the accountant up and the attorney, and our back taxes.

Accountants

When we first started the company Two Much Fun-N-A Boat, we needed an accountant. We first went to the firm where our attorney suggested. That firm helped us get started with filing the forms that needed to be filed with the Mexican government. They then filed a claim form every month that we were not in Mexico for us claiming zeroes of course because we weren't even there yet. After we arrived to live in Mexico and got things rolling, we went to the accounting firm and found out how much a month they were going to charge us. It was a lot of money per month and a lot of money that we did not have to spare or were not making at that time. Kevin's sister-in-law, Elvia, was an accountant; however, she did not do taxes for a living. She worked for a big company in Cancun and was really not familiar with all the tax laws. She did feel that she would be able to help us get started and file the zeroes for us for no charge. She was trying to help as best she could.

When we hired an employee, Captain Cesar, Elvia told us that there were certain forms that needed to be filled out and filed at the IMMS office. She got the forms for us, Kevin helped us fill them out, and then Laurel and I took them down to the IMMS office to file them. Bare in mind that this is a government office, and there was not a soul in that whole three-story building that could speak English. We found our way to the correct office and found our way to the correct person that we needed to hand the forms into, and we were on our way. Of course, we did not have a clue as to what we were doing, as usual, but we did it. Every time we added an employee or changed an employee, we had to go to this building and take care of the forms that needed filing. Most Americans that do business down there have an accountant that does these things for them. Not us. That would have been way too simple!

Elvia did the best that she could for us as long as she could, but I was getting a little concerned. About six months or so after we had moved there and started having tours, Lalo asked his brother-in-law, who is also an accountant, if he could help us out. He came over to my house in the evenings and tried to get things straightened out for us. Well, pretty soon, that became quite a task for him because he was so busy. I kept wanting to hire an accounting firm and kept harping about it. One of the times that I was in the United States on vacation, Laurel and Lalo went hunting for an accounting firm. They finally settled on one, and when I got back from the States, I was told about our new accountant. "Does he speak English?" was my first question.

"No" was the answer, "but Lalo can go with us when we need him to interpret."

Yeah, right! was my thought, but this is the accountant that we continued to go to for two years. After awhile we got to a point that we understood him, and we could speak to him also. However, I would get very frustrated quite often because I never really understood what was going on exactly. I had had accounting in high school and was very good at it. I did the daily accounting in the doctor's offices that I had worked in for twenty-one years. I could never understand why we never got a balance sheet, for one thing. We were actually getting one; it was just not what I had been used to looking at as a balance sheet. I was still doing the daily accounting, payroll, paying all our bills, etcetera, just not the month end stuff and figuring the taxes.

There are seven taxes alone for employees that we had to pay. A lot of time is spent every month gathering what is called a factura. This is an official receipt from every business that you buy anything for your business. A simple receipt is not sufficient. At the end of every month, you have to take all your receipts to the place that you have done business with for that month and get a factura. This means every time gas was purchased at different gas stations, you have to go back to that gas station for a factura. For all the supplies that we bought for the boat, we had to get a factura. You can get them the same day that you purchase the item; however, sometimes we were in too much of a hurry to wait in line or the factura office was closed at the time of purchase. There were many, many reasons why we ended up chasing all over town every month to get facturas. If we did not have facturas, we could not use the item as a business expense, and then the money came out of our pockets.

One day, I had to go to IMMS and file a paper for one of our employees that had quit. I went alone, and luckily, I took my English/Spanish dictionary with me. I got into the building, and I had to go to a different place than I usually had to go Therefore, I was not familiar with what to do at all. I was standing in a line that was all the way back to the end of the room! I was standing there, reading the signs at the three different windows. I thought that I was in the wrong line and kept reading and rereading the signs. I thought that I understood, but just in case, I pulled out my dictionary. Sure enough, I was in the really long line which had been the wrong line. I then moved to the correct window, and there was no one in line. I went up to the window, hoping not to make a fool out of myself. Sure enough, it was the correct window, and I got right through. Boy, I lucked out for a change. As I said, most offices would have their accountant to do these things, but unbeknownst to us, ours should have been doing so also.

Well, after two years of not really understanding what was going on, I pretty much insisted that we get an English-speaking accountant. We went to the first accounting office that we had dealt with. By this time, they were in a brand-new building and very expensive looking! Yup, they were! She wanted an ungodly amount every month, and there was no way we could afford to pay even though we were doing pretty good at that time. Laurel looked in the phone book and started calling firms and asking if they could speak English. She finally found a firm that had English-speaking accountants working there. We made an appointment, and yes, some could speak English, and yes, we could afford them. Yeah!

We had to have all our old accounting records sent from one firm to the next. We switched in January of 2005. They first had to go over all our old accounting records and make a report and then go from there. There were many things that we found out that were not being done that should have been done with the old firm. One big thing was that we were supposed to have been paying a city tax and had never. This had to be rectified because we also needed a city permit and had never had one. So we had to come up with quite a bit of money to pay back city taxes. We finally got straightened around after a few months, and things started to become a regular routine. Thank God we switched accountants! I was much happier knowing what in the world was going on with everything. It was still very frustrating for us, but it was getting easier.

Getting Ready to Leave Mexico

Laurel, Brittnay, and I had a girls' day by the pool at the Royal Islander on the April 10. It would be our last hurrah before I left. We had a friend who stayed at the Islander, and he had invited us to come and enjoy the pool. We had a good time, but it was also sad.

On one of the days right before I was leaving, Laurel and I approached the owner of the boat who had been renting our boat when his was full about buying our boat once again. This time, we had decided that we would take payments on the boat and trust him to complete the payments. Of course, we would have a contract drawn up for payments. He was very interested in our proposition; however, he had to speak with his American partner again. When I left Cancun, the boat was still sitting at the dock where it had been for our last tours, waiting to see if it would be sold.

On April 13, 2006, Trenton and I started packing in the early afternoon after taking the last load of my things to Laurel's house that I could not take with me because of lack of space. I was taking my kitchen table back with me because I could take the stand off and lay it flat in the bottom of my truck. Laurel got the four kitchen chairs. I had to leave a lot of my stuff with her, leaving her apartment packed to the gills! My truck cap leaked toward the front and in the back where it was damaged when I had been in the accident, so I took a huge tarp, put it down on the bottom of the truck, and planned on wrapping the tarp around my stuff once I got it all in my truck.

My ex-next-door neighbors came to bid me farewell and brought me a gift. Agusto ended up helping me pack with my other next-door neighbors looking on. We were trying to get my mattress and box springs into the truck but could not do so with the cap on my truck. My neighbor, Carlos, suggested that I take my truck for a little trip and get rid of my cap. In the end, that is exactly what I did! I could not get the bolts undone to release the cap, so I grabbed hold of the end of it and ripped it off. Carlos looked at me and said, "I'm glad I never tried to tangle with you!" We took a little drive and got rid of the cap, returned, and finished packing. By this time, Laurel and Brittnay had joined us and had helped get rid of the cap with me. After that, we did manage to get my mattress and box springs onto the load. Agusto then proceeded to help us tie everything down and put the buckle straps on. We got done shortly after dark. I bid Carla and Agusto good-bye, and they left. I did contact them last November of 2007 when I was down visiting, and Carla and I e-mail once in a while to keep in contact.

Armando and I had to say good-bye to each other also. This was very difficult, and many tears were shed by both of us. I did see him and spent a week with him when I was down in November of 2007, but he has since then moved back with his family in Guatemala whom he had not seen in almost fifteen years. I have not spoken to him since June of 2008. I guess he has moved on, and I am trying to do the same.

Trenton, Fargo, Pinata, and I left on Good Friday, April 14, 2006. I had purchased a new bed for both of them for their trip home (the dogs), not Trenton! I had left the backseat down this time and filled in the space from the backseat to the floor with a boat cushion rolled and tied on one side and my carry-on suitcase on the floor behind the passenger seat. Then I put another boat cushion on top of that and his big fat dog bed on top of that! He was lying on top of the world so to speak. He could lie there and look out the windows with ease. Piñata's bed was placed on the console between Trenton and I while Trenton was with me. We also had a lot of other things in the truck as well including some food for the boy! It is hard to keep a growing teenage boy full! My dash was full of maps, my folder containing all the papers from the truck accident in case I was accused of trying to escape an accident, my papers for the dogs from my veterinarian in Mexico with all their medical history and shot records, and mine and Trenton's legal documents.

I was running behind in the morning, leaving my house downstairs a mess. Laurel had told me the night before after we got through packing the truck not to worry about it and that she would take care of it. I left her the key to my house, and she later came back with Lalo and took down all the curtain rods with curtains that I had installed and took them to her house to put up. She also finished cleaning the living room and kitchen for me, so the house looked good when she was done. I had to go over to Laurel's to pick up Trenton and say good-bye to my daughter and granddaughter and Lalo. I almost missed Laurel as she was leaving to start her new job. She is now a PR for the Royal Resorts, and she loves what she is doing. She gets to see all our old customers who are always asking about my welfare as well as hers. We bid our farewells and started on our way.

I had decided to take the back road instead of the pay road as far as Merida and then got on the pay road. We stopped in Villadolid for lunch and had comida corrida. That means like our takeout food. I stayed in the truck with the dogs, and Trenton went for the food. We then stopped at a little park so that we could let the dogs out to rest, go to the bathroom, and relax a bit before we started up again. I had learned my lesson from the trip down. I now had purified water in a cooler with ice for Fargo at all times throughout the whole trip! We stopped quite often to let him out and move around and go to the bathroom. We stopped several times a day whenever I would see an open space so that he could move around. I did not wait until we needed gas or needed to eat. I was a little smarter this go-around. We got as far as Campeche the first night. We spent a lot of time in the town, driving around and looking for the same hotel that we had stayed at on the way down. I found it; we stopped to see if they still took dogs. They told me no, they did not take dogs, but the guy remembered me from four years ago and let us check in. He told me to keep the dogs hidden from everyone, which was a little difficult since Piñata insisted on barking at every little noise and thing! We spent the night uneventful and got an early start in the morning.

We had driven a couple of hours, and I got pulled over by a federale who was just checking to see what I had packed. He talked with us for a few minutes, looked the truck and load over, and let us be on our way. Then at the border check leaving Chiapas and entering Tabasco, I got stopped. The soldier asked for my license and registration; I gave them to him, and he walked away with them. He did not say anything, just walked away and went into a little shed-type building. He eventually looked out the window at me and motioned me in. I grabbed my folder with all my papers inside and went into his office. He was sitting there and in the process of writing me a ticket for speeding when entering into the zone. I started to argue with him in Spanish, which, I am sure, surprised him very much. I think that he thought he had a couple of gringos who would not be able to speak back to him in Spanish and would be so scared that we would just pay anything that he asked to get away. Well, he was very wrong. I told him that I had not been speeding and that I was almost at a stop before I entered their zone, which was a stop sign…*hello!*

He proceeded to tell me that the ticket amount was going to be forty-five pesos for each of his thirty men working at that time. I exploded and told him I did not have that kind of money on me and would not pay even if I did. After I got through with him, Trenton started in on him in his perfect Spanish with his Yucatán accent! The soldier told me that I was going to have to stay overnight in the Ciudad del Carmen and see the judge the next day. I reminded him that it was Saturday, and the next day was Easter Sunday! As we were arguing with him, Trenton kept going outside to check the truck and make sure no one was fooling with our stuff or trying to stuff drugs in the back of it or whatever.

Finally, the guy said to me, "Well, there are three things I can do, send you to jail, fine you, or let you off with a warning. I am going to let you off with a warning to slow down." We got out of there as fast as we could. I was trying to put my papers away, and Trenton told me to get out of there, and we could deal with the papers later! So we went! We made it to Villahermosa about 4:00 p.m. and started looking for a hotel. Every hotel that we stopped at was a hotel where you rent a room by the hour, if you know what I mean! Here is Trenton, running into these places and asking if they took dogs! After two hours of this, I got the heck out of there and started on our way looking for a place to stay. I ended up stopping at a gas station because my check engine light was on. I bought antifreeze and checked my oil but could not find anything wrong. There was a motel connected to the gas station, but they would not let us bring Fargo in even though he had been lying out on their grass the whole time that we had been at the station. They could see that he was very gentle but would not make an exception. I ended up driving through the night.

I stopped twice on the side of the road, the first time leaving the engine and air running for an hour while I slept, and the second time I shut the engine off but was only able to sleep for twenty minutes. As I was entering Veracruz, I came upon a huge entrance to something that I could not see because it was still dark. I shut off the truck and fell asleep until the sun started to rise, and Trenton woke up and thought that he was in paradise. We were actually parked in an entrance of a new subdivision that they were going to build. The only thing there was the entrance, palm trees planted, and a few bushes and rocks. We let the dogs out to run; Trenton ran for a bit himself, and then we started off. I knew we were very near the hotel that we had stopped at on our way down north of Veracruz. I drove through Veracruz and got out into the countryside a bit, and there was the place.

We stopped and asked if they still took dogs. Yes, they did, and they had a room available. It was Easter Sunday, and they were busy with many families there to enjoy Easter vacation. Armando had called me that morning to see if we were all right and how we were doing and where we were. It was good to hear his voice, and I was missing him terribly. We checked in at 10:30 a.m. I got the dogs settled. Trenton and I ate tuna and crackers and took showers, and then I took a nap. Trenton went out and about exploring and checking things out because he had slept all night. He came back into the room and woke me up only because I was not sleeping soundly enough. We did not do much during the rest of the day because there were a lot of people and kids in the pool, so I could not take Fargo anywhere near there. Fargo was always protective of kids in water; he did not like them in it! I sat out away from everyone, let him wander, and lay in the grass and just relaxed.

We all relaxed, and it sure felt good. Trenton did not care to go in the pool; I guess he was being shy. That does not happen very much with him, believe me! They had built a restaurant since we had been there the last time, so we put the dogs in our room and went to check out the restaurant for dinner. I did not see anything that appealed to me, so I did not order anything. I thought that Trenton had, however, so we were sitting there kind of just waiting. I had a cerveza, and I thought we were waiting for his food. After awhile, I asked him what in the world was taking so long for his food. He informed me that he had not ordered anything. We went back to the room and ate tuna and crackers again. We went to bed at 9:00 p.m. and slept soundly until Piñata woke us up at 6:30 a.m. barking at someone moving around. We got up and got ready to roll. We left and were on the road by 8:00 a.m. after eating cereal for breakfast.

I said a prayer, and we were on our way. I prayed for our safety every morning before even starting the engine. We got as far as Poza Rica, and then we got on the wrong road, and I mean road, not a street! It was full of holes and rocks and ended up through a god-awful, crowded pueblo. It was like they built all the houses and shops as close to the street as possible. Anyway, we got to a dead end, and we had to turn around and go back through the whole pueblo again, trying to squeeze my loaded truck down in between the buildings and all the people walking around in the pueblo. We ended up on another road after asking directions from an older man on the side of the road. He told Trenton of a shortcut to get back onto the Highway 180. This road was very interesting to say the least! We got back into the back country where there was *no* traffic, and we were driving on gravel sometimes, blacktop sometimes, and it was curvy and kind of scary after awhile when we did not get to the highway.

At one point in time, I was cruising about a whole 40 mph on blacktop when the road just dropped out from under me, and we dropped about ten feet! It is amazing that my load stayed on the truck and that the tires didn't pop or anything! We stopped the truck and got out to look to see if everything was still on the truck. Yes, everything was there, so we continued on. We got into some woodsy/jungle stuff and then came upon a little river. The old man had mentioned to Trenton that we would be crossing a river. This was good; however, he did not mention that we would actually be crossing a river without a bridge! Yes, we had to drive through a little streambed and up to the other side of it. We made that okay, and pretty soon, we were out on 180 once again. Thank God!

Trenton on his way to the US border with me as described in the book.

The road where it dropped off on our "shortcut" during the
trip back up to U.S. Border, described in the book.

Same road where it dropped off.

We stopped early that late afternoon and checked into a motel that did take dogs. They had a restaurant very close by within walking distance, and Trenton and I went there to eat after getting the dogs settled in the room. The people were very nice and very accommodating to us and to the dogs. It was very hot in the restaurant, but it was good to get something other than tuna! Trenton came up with the idea of getting up at 4:00 a.m. to get an early start, hoping to make it to Matamoros early enough to find the bus station, purchase his ticket back to Cancun, and get me across the border. He wanted to get back to Cancun within a day or two to spare before he had to start back to school again after Easter break. So this is what we did.

We got up at 4:00 a.m. and started on our way. The weather had been a little cooler in the night, therefore, creating fog and lots of it! The road we had to travel was very windy, woodsy, and *very* foggy. I drove through fog for about two hours or so, and then it started clearing as the sun was coming up. Trenton and I made it to the bus station in Matamoros approximately around

...opped and got gas, went in, got something ...ome more purified water for the dogs. We ...the bus station, and we found the bus station ...at all. Luckily, there was parking near the station ...et in the street of course. As I pulled my truck up to ... there was a bum begging and trying to wash my windows. ...yelled at him and told him to get away from my truck! Trenton was concerned about leaving my truck and going into the bus station to buy his tickets after that, but we had to do it.

I was able to buy both tickets for him at one time. The first was from Matamoros to Veracruz and Veracruz to Cancun. That was good because he did not have to carry a lot of cash with him and worry about getting robbed! He wanted the very best bus back. This included movies, reclining seats, bathroom, air, the whole nine yards. In order for him to get the bus that he wanted, he would have to wait at the bus station until 9:00 p.m. I asked the girl that was selling me the tickets if he would be safe sitting there in the bus station that long. She assured me that he would be just fine, so I let him have the ticket that he wanted. I gave him seven hundred pesos close to $70.00 U.S. for food for the trip home as he would have to grab food when the bus stopped for meals and to add people or let them off. I also was going to give him my cell phone. I had put five hundred pesos on it before we had left Cancun so that I could talk with Laurel and Armando and so that Trenton would be able to stay in contact with Laurel on his trip back home to Cancun. The original plan was for Trenton to go with me to the border, and then he would catch a taxi back to the bus station. The best laid plans don't always work out as we knew by now!

We drove as far and as close as it was possible for me to take him, and there was nothing there. No place for him to call or even hail a taxi. I had him get out and run across the highway and ask a guy that was walking along the road if there was a place that I could drop him closer to the border and he could call a taxi. The man told him, "No, there is no such place." This would be as far as he would be able to travel with me and not cross the border himself. So we turned around and headed back into the town a bit, and I thought that we could pull into the Chedraui there. That is a certain chain grocery store in Mexico. When we were on our way back from being near the border and heading to the parking lot at Chedraui, there were many people in wheelchairs with their families all out in the street, begging for money. They were catching the traffic that was just coming across from the United States. I took him over to the side by the bus stops, and we said our good-byes. I suggested to him that he catch a bus back to the bus station. He just looked at me as if I were insane, and he said, "Grandma, I would be the only gringo on the bus in a border town all by myself. That would not be a good idea!" Okay, what did I know; he was the streetwise child, not me! He was going to have to cross the street and try to hail a taxi.

I can't believe I just left him there and that I did not even wait until he was safely in a taxi, but I didn't. I was not thinking straight, obviously! I was so worried about crossing the border. All I could think of was that I was going to have to unpack the truck and then try to repack it all by myself! Before I left Trenton, I had called Laurel and told her good-bye and started crying. I then called Armando and told him good-bye and started crying again. Then when I said my good-byes to Trenton, I started crying once again. I headed across after leaving Trenton, and I was so nervous about leaving Trenton and about crossing. I made it to the first stop where they run your passport through the machine. Then I was told I would have to pull over to the side where they could check my truck. There were two men and one woman standing there, waiting for me. I stopped the truck, put my window down, and the first thing out of my mouth was, "I'm so glad that you have dogs to check my stuff!" They could see that I had been crying, and I am sure they could tell that I was very nervous. They were all very nice to me, and the guy with the dog noticed that I had dogs with me, so he walked across the street, down the street, and approached my truck from behind. That was so nice because my dogs didn't even know that there was another dog around.

While I was driving across, Fargo was in the back lying on all his cushions as comfy as can be, snoring! He woke up when one of the guys came to the passenger side window and started talking to Piñata and to Fargo and to me about the dogs. When he did that, I started to calm down and relaxed. He stood there chitchatting with me the whole time that they were checking my truck , I assume, because I could not see a thing I was so loaded down. After only about ten minutes, they told me that I could go. Whew! That was easy! I was good to go and so wanted to kiss the ground of the good ole United States of America!

I crossed the border on Wednesday and drove only a few towns north into Texas before I stopped. It was early, but I needed to get out and relax and chill out. The motel that I stayed at had a big open field connected to it, so I was able to let my dogs run for quite a bit. Well, Piñata did a lot of running; Fargo just walked around, smelling and marking, and just happy to be out of the truck. The following day, I was up early, and we were on our way. My plans were to change the route that my brother had mapped out for me. He had me going right through Houston, and I did not particularly want to drive through Houston. I still had my original directions from when we drove down, so I thought that I could just reverse those and be good. I started off okay, but the road that I was on just petered out, and I ended up on the expressway heading toward Houston. *No!*

I stopped at a rest area, of which there are not many, not like Michigan anyway. I got my maps out, my directions, the dogs, their water, a dish and their food. I went over where there were some big oak trees and let the dogs loose, and there was no one else in the whole place, and I started studying my maps. We were there for quite a while, and this guy came and was sitting far away from me on a kind of cement wall–type thing just looking around and watching my dogs. Then a car pulled in as I was busy looking at my map; a guy and his dog got out. My little Piñata went flying over toward them when she saw the other dog! I jumped up, told Fargo to stay, and went with a leash after Piñata. I got her, apologized to the man with the dog, and went back to my trees and Fargo. I soon decided that there was nothing else I could do but drive through Houston. I gathered all my stuff and headed for my truck. The one guy was still sitting there and watched me put the dogs in the truck and everything else away. He then said something to me, and I told him that I was headed north and did not want to drive through Houston and was trying to figure out a way not to do so. He asked me if I had my maps and directions and told me that he was a truck driver and maybe could help. So I took my maps and directions over to him.

He looked at the route my brother had planned for me to go through Houston and told me that I definitely did not want to go that way. He said that he lived in Houston and drove a truck in the area all the time. So he then showed me a better way to go and told me exactly how many tollbooths that I would go through before getting off the toll road. So I got in the truck after thanking him. I then thanked the good Lord for sending another angel when I needed one. We were off with much tribulation in my stomach and driving very carefully. As I approached Houston, the toll road that I ended up on was I think at least six lanes, and it really seems that it was about eight lanes. Maybe it was because I was driving in unfamiliar territory with such a load on my truck.

When I came upon the first tollbooth, of course I was in the wrong lane! All of the lanes were open to those who had daily passes or correct change. I, of course, had neither. Therefore, I had to work my way over to the far right. This might seem like an easy task but not when traffic is flying by and your truck is so full inside and out! I made it through the three tollbooths just like the man had told me to do, got off on the correct highway, and was on my way to Arkansas to see my brother and sister-in-law and a little R & R. That night, I was still in Texas and found a very nice Holiday Inn to stay in for the night around 7:30p.m. She put us right at poolside, which surprised me because of having the dogs with me. It worked out very nice because I was able to leave the dogs in the room while I went to the pool and swam and relaxed my poor body some.

We were in northern Texas, and behind the hotel there were some big pine trees along the side and a huge open field. When I got unpacked, I took the dogs out back to run and relax. It seemed to me that when Fargo was sniffing around the pines and in the pine needles, I could see him perk up like he knew at that time he was headed back home to Michigan. You probably think I am crazy or imagining it, but I think it is true. He knew! That made me very happy to see him perk up like that. I kept asking God to please just let me get him back to Michigan. Actually, he was doing so much better on the trip home. He was drinking purified water and getting out about every two hours to walk a little, drink, and relax a bit. He really spent most of his time snoring in the backseat with all his cushions and big bed. He did not spend the time anxiously or panting as he had on the trip down.

The next morning, I was up at 6:30 a.m. and on the road by 7:30 a.m. I hit a heavy rain, but later, the sun came out, and my mattress dried out. You see, I did not have a tarp on my load. I had been very lucky with the weather so far. That previous night while I was at the Holiday Inn, it sprinkled, so I just took the tarp, put it on top and around the load, used some tie-downs, and called it good for the night. I uncovered it before I took off the next morning. I got to my brother's house at 6:00 p.m. I had watched my odometer roll over to 150,000 miles, 25 miles south of Little Rock, Arkansas. My red check engine light had gone off somewhere in Mexico.

On Friday morning, I got up at 8:00 a.m. This is the latest I had slept my whole seven days of traveling. It was good to be at my brother's. I slept so good. It is very beautiful where he had built his house and very peaceful and quiet. The dogs and I needed a break after driving for seven days straight. We just relaxed the whole day and talked. Fargo ate more than he had eaten the whole trip up so far! I took my brother and sister-in-law out to dinner that evening, and then we took a drive around one of the camp grounds on the Shoals and then returned back to his house. I checked my e-mail to see if I had anything from Laurel. The next morning, Keith was up around 6:30 a.m. and out covering my truck up so that nothing would get wet the rest of the trip home. I joined him around 7:30 a.m. and crawled underneath the truck to tie some of the ropes down. We then went in the house and had a wonderful breakfast of ham, eggs, potatoes, and toast. This probably was the most that I had eaten since I left Mexico as I still had been eating my cereal and tuna. I had stopped at a grocery store in Texas and replenished my supplies. After breakfast, Keith and I went back out in his pole barn to finish up what we had started before breakfast. We finally finished around noon. We had lunch, and then Keith lay down for a nap. Joanna had washed all my dirty clothes for me and hung them out in the wonderful breeze that was blowing. I washed both the dogs as it was a warm and beautiful sunny day. We spent the rest of the day being lazy and relaxing.

The next day was Sunday, April 23, 2006. I packed up everything, all my clean clothes, dog stuff, and was on the road at 10:00 a.m. I made it as far as Indiana, and my "check engine soon" light started coming on and off again as it had in Mexico. It was getting late, around 10:00 p.m., and I was approaching Indianapolis, Indiana. I wanted to try to get through there so that I would not have to deal with the heavy traffic on Monday morning. My truck was not running right by then, and I tried to trust in the Lord that he would get me through that large city before something happened and the truck stopped running altogether. I made it through and pulled off in the second little town just north of Indianapolis. By this time, it was very late, 11:30 p.m., and there was nothing open. I pulled into a place with little cabins. They had all the lights out and a closed sign on the office door. My truck was making such a terrible noise by then; I dared not try to go further.

So I took the dogs out to go potty, and we settled in for the night. I did not have a blanket or anything in my truck to cover up with. I had shorts on because when I had left Arkansas, it was warm! Now it was around forty degrees! Shortly after we tried to settle down, the owner came out to see why I was sitting there in her parking lot. I told her what the problem was, and she took me inside the office and rented me a room—another angel. The next morning, I was up early, and it was freezing! I took the dogs out to potty and then crawled under my truck to see if one of the ropes that I had tied had maybe come untied and wrapped around something under there. I didn't know; it was just a guess on my part! Wrong guess! The ropes were still all okay.

A man was at the hotel that worked there and was outside smoking. I asked him about a mechanic. He knew of one; he told me that the guy used to be a mechanic at the GM dealer and then started his own place of business. He called him for me and let me talk to him. I told him what the problem was, and he gave me directions to his place of business, which was in the town just south of where I was. I tried starting my truck, but it wouldn't start. I called the guy back, and he told me he would be right there to pick my truck up with his wrecker. So he came within a short period, picked up the truck, my dogs, and I, and drove us all to his shop. He told me that it sounded like a fuel pump. He put my truck up on the hoist right away. I had told him where I had come from and where I was headed, so he got to me right away so as not to cause any more delays as possible.

There was a huge open field connected to his place that he owned, so I took the dogs over there and let them loose while we waited. I was back on the road by 11:30 a.m., and we were on our way once again. Talk about being blessed! I was extremely tired, and I fell asleep four times at the wheel. The fourth time I woke up, I happened to be driving over water. I decided right then that I had better pull over before we were all swimming! I slept for a while, and then we were on our way. The dogs and I arrived back in Bay City, Michigan, at 6:00 p.m. on Monday, April 24, 2006! I drove directly to my house to let my renter know that I was in town and ready to move in as soon as possible. It just so happened that she had a moving company coming the next day and said that she would be out of my house that day also. Yes!

I then drove over to Leslie's house. That is where the dogs and I had planned to stay until my house was empty. It was really nice that we only had to spend one night and then be able to get into my house. The next morning, we woke up early, and the first place I had to go was to the local pet store and buy Piñata a sweater because it was only in the forties, and my poor Cancun puppy was freezing to death! I bought a sweater for her and then went to my home and worked out in the yard most of the day, raking and burning leaves and twigs and tree limbs. I just enjoyed being out in my yard in the wide-open spaces so to speak and doing what I liked to do. I tied Piñata up as she had that street tendency to wander and not come when she was called. Fargo, I am sure, was tickled pink to be back in his own yard too!

When I knew that I was coming back to my home, I would lie in bed in Cancun at night, thinking of all the things that I wanted to do to my house. It did not take me long to get things started, and it kept me busy until good riding weather came. I snagged my neighbor next door to me to help me move my bed into my house. He helped me carry the mattress and box springs in. I did the rest. I had everything unloaded within a half hour and got my bed set up and made. I put my kitchen table together and brought in my plastic deck chairs to sit in. This was all the furniture that I had except the dressers that I had stored at Leslie's house in her basement. I had to start from scratch and pay for my house once again at the ripe ole age of fifty-nine. I was so happy to be back home, I cannot tell you!

When I left Mexico, the boat was still at the same dock that we had been using at the last. However, as we were no longer running with tours, she needed to be moved where we did not have to pay. Once again, our dear friend Carlos told Laurel that she could move the boat to his marina and try to sell it from there. It may sound like a simple thing to do, but of course, it wasn't. Mundo Marina is on the lagoon side of Cancun. This meant that the mast had to be dropped to get the boat under the bridge and into the lagoon. Laurel went to Palemon and asked him if he would help her do this. She offered to pay him, but all he wanted was cab fair to get there. She also asked Jose to help, and he agreed to do so also. So she had herself, Palemon, Jose, and Trenton. The instructions for this boat to be put back together states that you must have a crane available to raise the mast. These four had no problem dropping the mast. When they got it to the marina, the hard job began. They tried to use one of the palm trees as a hoist. They had tourists stopping on the sidewalk to watch the process. This process took them seven or eight hours, and what a struggle it was!

Some of the marina workers were helping as well. They got the job done; the mast was back up. Praise the Lord! The boat was never sold. When I had gone down the following November, Laurel and I approached Carlos and asked if we could give him the boat. He was very gracious to us as always and said that he had been thinking of using her in the lagoon for sunset tours out of his restaurant. We told him that we thought that would be an excellent idea; in fact, we had thought of doing something like that for quite some time if we would ever have gotten ahead. So he agreed to take her. Shortly after that, we had an AD on the Internet, and someone called me about the boat. I told him that he would have to call Carlos as he was the owner of the boat. He did, and Carlos told him to do his dealing with the girls. All he wanted out of it was his dock fee even though we had given him the boat. To make another long story short, the deal fell through, and Carlos is still stuck with the boat. She is still sitting at his dock, taking up space that I am sure he could use. What a wonderful man he is and a very dear friend to two strangers from the United States. May God continue to bless you, Carlos! As you walk by Mundo Marina or take a tour from there, look at the end of the dock to the left. There you will see the *Pollo Primavera* in all her pink and purple glory.

Laurel is still selling time-shares for the Royal Resorts. Brittnay got hired in also selling time shares but has since been let go. Brittnay has just recently been hired by the Royal Caribbean Cruise Line to work up in Denali, Alaska, at one of their hotels. She will be moving directly from Cancun, Mexico, up to Denali, Alaska. Quite a change, and we are praying that this will be a great opportunity for her. Trenton is finishing up tenth grade this year. He turns seventeen in a few weeks at the end of February. He is also ready to move back to the States and hopes to go to college here in the United States. Laurel is on the verge of being ready to move back. She still is not doing as financially well as she had hoped. The US economy right now is suffering, so therefore, so is she. If she moved back, she will be really starting from scratch. Only God knows what he has in store for our future. They were all able to come back home for Christmas. It was a wonderful Christmas; the best we have had since my husband, their dad, died. Laurel got to see a lot of family while they were here, and most importantly, she got to see her brother. They do miss each other very much.

Palemon was able to add on to his house and almost double the size while he was working for us. He is now the full-time captain of the *Sea Passion*, of which Laurel and I always referred to as the *Sea Witch*. On a good day, he will have as many as one hundred people aboard. His oldest daughter, Carla, is now in high school and is going to a "pay" school to receive a better education.

She is now learning English. We wish only the best for him and always had such high hopes of helping him and his family. I had dreams of one day sending him and his whole family to Disney World in Florida.

Those are the kind of dreams that Laurel and I had when we moved down there. We had no intentions of becoming millionaires as a lot of the boat owners are or close. We only wanted to live down there, make a good living, and be able to help some of the people whom we came in contact. Inadvertently, we did help a lot of people. Mostly because we were taken advantage of, and that is not how we intended to do it!

Laurel's car was no longer running. The last mechanic that she paid 800 US dollars to replace the transmission only took her money, and that was pretty much all he did. They tried to get the police involved to get him to fix it, but all that accomplished was he came and took the engine apart, left everything sitting out on the street, and left. The car is still sitting on some street with no more hopes of moving again. She has over three hundred thousand miles on her, so I guess that is pretty much it. Laurel has been without a car for almost a year now. She takes the bus along with all the other poor Mexicans.

People ask me all the time, "Would you do it all over again?" This is a very difficult question to answer. As you have read, living down there was very difficult for us. We went through a lot of hardships and bad experiences. However, we went through a lot of neat experiences and met a tremendous amount of very cool people and people from all over the world. We were all bilingual and have experienced another culture. Our faith is so much stronger. So would I do it again? Financially, no! Other than the financial part of it, I would probably say yes. I guess it is for everyone to judge whether they would put themselves through those things again. To me, it is better to be able to think about all the things that we went through than to sit on my deck someday in my rocking chair thinking about "Gee, if we had only done that, I wonder what would have happened." I guess this says it all. We also feel that maybe this is what God intended for us all along. After all, I did have a lot more time to sit and read the Bible. We also made a big difference in a lot of people's lives there as they did ours. All of us knew that we didn't need a lot of things to make us happy; they are just things. Family is what is important. I am still trying to recover financially and probably never will, but I sure am glad to be back in the United States.

I am now anxiously awaiting another trail riding season with my horse and dogs. May God bless you all for buying my book and reading our little story. Onto the next adventure in life!

Laurel's Car

As I had stated in the beginning, Laurel has a 1997 Cavalier that she drove down to Mexico. This car has been a very amazing car. It keeps taking licks and keeps on ticking! Shortly after we were there, her friend Juan was driving her car. They had gone to the post office or something, anyway, when he was backing out of his parking spot he swung the car and slammed the right fender right into a cement slab. At least it was a cement slab and not someone else's car!

There was the time in between tours that we were coming from the hotel zone and were stopped at the light just before you enter Tulum Avenue. If you have been there, you probably know what I am talking about. It kind of goes around in a circle like the circles you see in films in other foreign countries. The circle has four entrances and exits, which are main streets. Anyway, we needed to go left and go to my house to make snacks for the second tour of the day. The light turned, and she continued forward and started swinging toward the left. As we were doing this, other traffic was coming into the circle and trying to beat their red light. A taxi came right alongside of our right side and clipped her right in the right side of the front area around her headlight. The taxi driver jumped out of the car and started yelling at us. Of course, by then, we could pretty much yell back in Spanish and defend ourselves. Before you could blink an eye, almost, we had four different transitó cars there on the scene. None of them spoke any English.

Laurel immediately called Lalo. Once again, Lalo to the rescue! Tada! The poor guy shows up, and first has to listen to us rant and rave about the dumb taxi driver and then has to listen to the taxi driver and the police! It would have been enough to drive him to drink, don't you think? The taxi driver wanted us to pay cash up front and of course "a little" for all the transitó standing around. He told Laurel what they wanted, and she hit the roof. We were not at fault, and doggone it, we were not going to pay! Lalo told the taxi driver that he might just as well forget it because he knew Laurel, and if she said that she was not going to pay, then she would not pay! He told him that we had all day to go down to the transitó building and argue it out down there if it took us all day long. Lalo finally convinced the guy to forget getting money from us, and he (the taxi driver) had to slip the transitós a little something himself! That is one time that we were not the ones shelling out the pesos. However, Laurel's car had another dent in it. We ended up missing the second tour, and the guys had to handle things themselves. We met the boat when it came in in the evening and explained to the people what had happened.

At another time, Laurel had had her car repaired by a mechanic that I had been using and trusted. I met his wife one day out walking Fargo, and she was walking her rottweilers also. We got to talking, and she was from Germany. She had come to Cancun many years ago on vacation, met her husband, and got married. Anyway, I trusted this guy because we became friends. He had done lots of work on my truck by then, so Laurel took her car to him when she needed a new generator. Her car had actually stopped running on the street that I lived on, and she had to leave it parked there. The mechanic was not very far away from my house, so he came over to take a look at it. He said it needed a new generator and that he would have to pick it up. Laurel had to give him the money to buy it, and when he got it, he came back and installed it.

A few weeks or months later, I cannot remember exactly and it really does not matter, she started having problems with the car again. I happened to be in the States at the time, so I did not actually see this happen, but I saw the car later. The wonderful mechanic and "friend" put in a generator for a Chrysler boat engine, and the thing caused her car to explode, which caused the airbags to go off. It just so happened that Lalo was in the car at the time; the air bag hit him in the face and broke the windshield of the car, and Lalo had to go to the doctor for his face. When I got back from the States, I went with Laurel to pick up her car and take it to have a new windshield put in. There was glass all over the seat of her car, front and back; there was a hole in the middle of the steering wheel where the air bag had been and a hole in the dashboard where the other air bag had been. Her car still looks like that today! We had no money to fix anything other than to keep them running. Needless to say, we had to find another mechanic and started going to (once again) a cousin of Kevin's. Actually, he was Hanna's cousin. He spoke no English, but that was okay because by then we were okay in Spanish. So my knowledge in Spanish revolves around banking, accounting, boating, and car mechanics!

Present Time: November 2012

S ince it has been four to five years from the time that I completed my book and getting around to getting it published, I thought that an update on everyone would be in order.

Laurel is now married to Lalo; they got married in September of 2009. They are both back in the States and have been for one and a half years. Laurel had been working part time and just got a full-time position at a company with a lot of growth potential. She is also going to school to complete her degree as an accountant. She just received her associate degree this spring, graduating with highest honors with a 3.98 GPA. I had to put this in here as I am very proud of her. She should graduate with her bachelors in 2014.

Lalo has his papers to work legally, is working as a waiter, and now has his green card.

Brittnay returned from Alaska and moved to Buffalo, New York, for a while and was working in merchandise sales. She is now back in Michigan and has been working with a company for three years, utilizing her Spanish. She has also started college and is getting her associate degree in vet tech medicine with thoughts of getting her bachelor's degree in criminal justice.

Trenton has joined the US army and graduated from boot camp in September of 2012 and is now finishing up his job training in Virginia. He will then get to come home with us for two weeks before being shipped over to Germany. From Germany he will be going to Afghanistan. He came back in his last year of high school, lived with me, and completed high school here in the United States giving him more opportunities. He had been working for the fire department in Cancun and also as a paramedic for an ambulance company. He had studied through the Red Cross down in Cancun and received his certification through the Red Cross. He has seen and done quite a lot in his twenty-one years, and I am sure he has just begun!

Armando still calls me to see how I am and let me know how he is doing. However, I have not heard from him in about a year so I am hoping that he has finally met someone else, fallen in love and is going on with his life.

Ruth. When I got back from Cancun, I pretty much resumed my life as it were with cleaning houses again, riding my horse, going to my little church that I had missed so very much, and hanging out with my sister. She has since passed away with cancer. I am so very thankful that I came back when I did and was able to spend her last few years with her. I now have a horse trailer with partial living quarters (no more tenting). I lost Fargo after being back for a year and now have another great dane whose name is Pancho. I still have Piñata and she adjusted quite well to the Michigan weather although she still goes out in 90-degree weather and lays in the sun for a bit. I have a new horse that was given to me a couple of years ago, and I named him Regalo, which means "gift" in Spanish. Thankfully, he came in at a time that I needed to retire my old horse, and he is working out beautifully for me. I spent one winter training him, so he is truly mine. I sold my old smashed in truck and bought a new three-quarter ton to haul my bigger trailer with in 2007. I have plans on totally retiring from cleaning houses in May 2013. My next dream is to travel with my horse and dogs to the southern states in the winter and trail ride in Michigan and the surrounding states all summer long.

Trenton diving into water at a cenote in Tisamin.

Ruth sitting at a cenote in Leona Vicario.